Ensuring Parental Rights of Military Service Academy Cadets and Midshipmen

Policy and Cost Implications

LAURA L. MILLER, STEPHANIE RENNANE, JAIME L. HASTINGS, ANTHONY JACQUES, TARA LAILA BLAGG, DANIEL B. GINSBERG, BARBARA BICKSLER

Prepared for the Office of the Secretary of Defense
Approved for public release; distribution unlimited

RAND NATIONAL DEFENSE RESEARCH INSTITUTE

For more information on this publication, visit **www.rand.org/t/RRA2059-1**.

Published by the RAND Corporation, Santa Monica, Calif.

Library of Congress Cataloging-in-Publication Data is available for this publication.

ISBN: 978-1-9774-1072-6

Cover: Ramona/CrochethookersGifts.

About This Report

As of late 2022, U.S. Department of Defense (DoD) policy prohibits cadets and midshipmen at the U.S. military service academies (MSAs) from having dependents while enrolled, meaning these undergraduates are not allowed to have "a legally recognized obligation to provide support" to anyone, including a spouse or child.[1] The demands of parenthood are treated as incompatible with the demands of life at the MSAs. Cadets or midshipmen who have become parents while enrolled have been required to sever their legal obligation to support the child, resign from the academy, or face disenrollment. The fiscal year (FY) 2022 National Defense Authorization Act (NDAA) requires a change to this policy, directing that the Secretary of Defense prescribe regulations that provide options for cadets and midshipmen who become biological parents while enrolled at an MSA to retain parental rights while maintaining their other individual and academic responsibilities.[2]

To help inform this policy change, the Office of the Under Secretary of Defense for Personnel and Readiness, Manpower and Reserve Affairs, commissioned the RAND National Defense Research Institute in FY 2022 to characterize the legal, policy, practice, and cost implications of changing DoD's MSA rules to comply with the FY 2022 NDAA, as well as make recommendations on associated changes in policies and practices. This research report describes the project's approach, findings, conclusions, and recommendations.

The research reported here was completed in January 2023 and underwent security review with the sponsor and the Defense Office of Prepublication and Security Review before public release.

RAND National Security Research Division

This research was sponsored by the Office of the Under Secretary of Defense for Personnel and Readiness, Manpower and Reserve Affairs and conducted within the Personnel, Readiness, and Health Program of the RAND National Security Research Division (NSRD), which operates the National Defense Research Institute (NDRI), a federally funded research and development center sponsored by the Office of the Secretary of Defense, the Joint Staff, the Unified Combatant Commands, the Navy, the Marine Corps, the defense agencies, and the defense intelligence enterprise.

[1] Department of Defense Instruction 1322.22, *Service Academies*, U.S. Department of Defense, September 24, 2015, pp. 10, 21.

[2] Public Law 117-81, National Defense Authorization Act for Fiscal Year 2022, Section 559A, Regulations on Certain Parental Guardianship Rights of Cadets and Midshipmen, December 27, 2021.

For more information on the RAND Personnel, Readiness, and Health Program, see www.rand.org/nsrd/prh or contact the director (contact information is provided on the webpage).

Acknowledgments

We would like to thank the many individuals who contributed to and supported this research. First, we thank our project monitors from Accession Policy: Lt Col Julie Anne Rudy (Assistant Director, Officer Commissioning Programs) and Dennis J. Drogo (Assistant Director, M&RA/Military Personnel Policy).

Several individuals generously helped identify policies, regulations, practices, and resources that might need to be changed to support implementation of the FY 2022 NDAA requirement regarding the parental rights of military service academy cadets and midshipmen or provided supporting information and data needed for our analyses. These individuals include

- Office of the Secretary of Defense (OSD): Jeri Busch (OSD Compensation) and James Fasano and Alicia Litts (OSD Comptroller's Office)
- Department of the Air Force: Dominic Angiollo and Dixon Dykman (U.S. Air Force Academy)
- Department of the Army (DOA): LTC Shanna Hendrix (DOA) and LTC Brian Novoselich and CPT Marshall Greenberg (U.S. Military Academy)
- Department of the Navy (DON): LCDR Gray Guthrie (DON) and CAPT David Forman and Maj Vicky Crabbe (U.S. Naval Academy).

We also thank our RAND colleagues Melissa Baumann and Andrea Wiernik for their support with this report. Additionally, Molly McIntosh and Kirsten Keller provided excellent feedback on our interim research products and previous versions of this report. We are also grateful for the thoughtful quality assurance review by retired U.S. Air Force Lt Gen Brian T. Kelly. Finally, Jim Powers provided advice that helped us improve the flow, clarity, and effectiveness of the report.

Summary

Issue

U.S. Department of Defense (DoD) policy prohibits cadets and midshipmen at the U.S. military service academies (MSAs) from having dependents while enrolled.[3] Cadets or midshipmen who have become parents while enrolled have been required to sever their legal obligation to support the child, resign from the academy, or face disenrollment. However, the fiscal year (FY) 2022 National Defense Authorization Act (NDAA) requires that the Secretary of Defense change this policy so that cadets and midshipmen who become parents while attending an MSA can preserve their parental rights, "consistent with the individual and academic responsibilities of such cadet or midshipman."[4]

To help inform this policy change, the Office of the Under Secretary of Defense for Personnel and Readiness, Manpower and Reserve Affairs commissioned the RAND National Defense Research Institute to characterize the legal, policy, practice, and cost implications of changing DoD's MSA rules to comply with the FY 2022 NDAA.

Approach

We used multiple methods to explore the potential implications of allowing cadets and midshipmen to retain parental rights while enrolled. We reviewed state laws and statutes related to parental rights and responsibilities, particularly regarding the termination of parental rights. We reviewed relevant military-specific federal laws and DoD, military department, and MSA policies and procedures. We met with senior representatives from the Office of the Secretary of Defense, military departments, and MSAs both to identify relevant policies, regulations, and practices to consider and to solicit relevant demographic and cost data. Our cost analyses relied on the best available data and considered multiple policy options that could be debated by the public; policymakers; military leaders; and cadets, midshipmen, and their families.

Key Findings

We break down our key findings by category in the following sections.

---

[3] Department of Defense Instruction (DoDI) 1322.22, *Service Academies*, U.S. Department of Defense, September 24, 2015, pp. 10, 21.

[4] Public Law 117-81, National Defense Authorization Act for Fiscal Year 2022, Section 559A, Regulations on Certain Parental Guardianship Rights of Cadets and Midshipmen, December 27, 2021.

Policy Implications

- Changing DoD policy to allow cadets and midshipmen to preserve their parental rights has implications for policies on a host of issues. DoD's policy options include minimally complying with the FY 2022 NDAA; creating guidance to ensure consistent implementation; providing benefits, programs, and services that match or more closely mirror those provided to other active-duty personnel; and lifting other related prohibitions on marriage, having children on entering, or having other types of dependents. At the time of this writing, DoD's approach is consistent with creating guidance to ensure consistent implementation, with the relevant DoDI expected to be updated in 2023.[5]
- DoD has many policy options, but even if it does not provide substantial additional benefits to cadet and midshipman parents, it is highly unlikely that state courts would require involuntary termination of the parental rights of cadets and midshipmen on the grounds of too little financial support or not enough time spent with their children. State laws strongly uphold parental rights.
- The Servicemembers Civil Relief Act may temporarily shield cadets and midshipmen who are sued by their co-parents for custody or financial support.[6] However, these cadets and midshipmen could still incur significant legal expenses.

Cost Implications

- A lack of data makes it difficult to estimate both the scope and the cost implications of various policy options. At the time of this writing, there is no requirement to collect data on how many cadets and midshipmen become parents each year. As a result, no reliable and centralized data source contains information on cadet and midshipmen who are parents or on their academic outcomes.
- The potential costs of the various policy options for an individual parent depend on several factors, such as whether the cadet or midshipman is the one who becomes pregnant and when in their academic career they become parents (e.g., in their first or fourth year of school). The latter affects how many years of support costs would be necessary.
- Aggregated costs will depend on the total number of parents and distribution of parent characteristics (e.g., biological mother or father, leave-of-absence patterns), which are unknown. To understand the potential magnitude of total costs, we modeled aggregate costs for ten parents in a given cohort over the course of their tenure at the academy. Aggregate costs ranged from $33,000 to $1.8 million across the various scenarios we modeled.
- Costs could be characterized as sizable for an individual but small in the aggregate. In the scenarios we modeled, costs to DoD for various policy options could be a significant

[5] DoDI 1322.22, 2015, pp. 10, 21.

[6] U.S. Code, Title 50, War and National Defense; Chapter 50, Servicemembers Civil Relief; Section 3902, Purpose.

share of the cost of four years of education for one cadet or midshipman (i.e., 3–58 percent), while aggregate costs could be a small share of the approximately $1.4 billion cost of four years of education for a graduating cohort (i.e., less than 1 percent in our hypothetical scenario). Total health care costs could also be a small share of the approximately $72 million cost of four years of TRICARE health care costs for an entire cohort (i.e., less than 1 percent in our hypothetical scenario).

- Our models are based on scenarios in which cadets and midshipmen continue to live in dorms on campus and do not have physical custody of their children. Evaluating the policy and cost implications of changes to housing options at the MSAs would require a more comprehensive effort than was feasible within this project to understand implications for the parents and their fellow students, as well as logistics and feasibility at the academies.

Recommendations

- **DoD should adopt policy options for cadets and midshipmen that are consistent with its policies for other active-duty personnel, leveraging the strengths of its Military Family Readiness System.**[7] Additional pay, benefits, and other supports could be offered to help ensure cadet and midshipman health, well-being, and ability to focus on professional and academic responsibilities; to address inequities across students; and to attract and retain quality officers. For example,
  - the availability of some or all of the additional supports could be linked to an earlier service commitment (i.e., in the first or second year at the academy) or a longer service obligation after graduation
  - DoD-assisted transfer to the Reserve Officers' Training Corps with a scholarship could also help keep quality candidates in the officer pipeline and provide greater flexibility for them to exercise their parental rights
  - DoD could also establish a program to allow cadets and midshipmen who are becoming parents to move to enlisted status for a set period during which they could earn better pay and receive full benefits for themselves and their child and then either request academy readmission or fulfill an enlisted term of service.[8]
- **DoD, the military departments, and the MSAs should create detailed policies on MSA practices related to pregnancy, childbirth, and postpartum care.** Senior leader guidance could help prevent inconsistency and dangerous or discriminatory actions.

7 DoDI 1342.22, *Military Family Readiness*, U.S. Department of Defense, August 5, 2021; Kenneth W. Kizer and Suzanne Le Menestrel, eds., *Strengthening the Military Family Readiness System for a Changing American Society*, National Academies Press, 2019.

8 As discussed in Chapter 3, each academy has a mentorship program that could serve as a model for this enlisted option.

The forthcoming update to the 2015 DoDI 1322.22 for the service academies is expected to provide higher-level guidance on physical fitness requirement adjustments. More local guidance will be needed to manage such issues as logistics for prenatal medical appointments, permissions for fathers to attend childbirth, and accommodations for pregnancy and postpartum needs (such as morning sickness and lactation).

- **In the short term, DoD should take some basic steps to help ensure the health and well-being of cadets and midshipmen who are becoming parents and of their children.** This can be accomplished by providing leave with health care for a cadet's or midshipman's period of pregnancy, childbirth, and postpartum care, as well as health care coverage for the child. It appears that DoD could make this change because cadets and midshipmen are categorized as active-duty personnel in some respects, and U.S. Code does not prohibit their children from receiving health care, like children of other active-duty personnel do. However, Section 559A of the FY 2022 NDAA does not explicitly address this issue,[9] and the law does at times call out cadets and midshipmen as exceptions to active-duty personnel requirements,[10] so additional legislative clarity may be needed to confirm or provide eligibility.
- **DoD and the MSAs should develop and implement plans to ensure that applicants, as well as cadets and midshipmen, understand new policies regarding their parental rights and responsibilities.** This plan should include any local, state, federal, or military resources available to support cadet and midshipman parents; options for continuing or discontinuing enrollment and potential recoupment; and applicable associated policies (e.g., leave policies, policies regarding pregnancy). The plan should include direct communication with students and a publicized repository of such information that is easily accessible to cadets and midshipmen.
- **DoD should conduct or support further qualitative research to evaluate possible changes to housing, child development centers, and cadet and midshipman privileges.** Any proposed changes to allow cadets and midshipmen who are parents to use MSA family housing or child development centers or to have other privileges that their peers do not have (e.g., have a car, miss activities, leave campus to visit their child) need to be thoroughly explored and carefully considered before being adopted.
- **While new and revised policies are being established, DoD and the MSAs should collect, monitor, and analyze data on the parenthood status of cadets and midshipmen.**
  - The data analyses should be used to better understand the size and demographic characteristics of this group; patterns related to their enrollment, performance, and retention; potential signs of disparate impact; whether additional supports or guid-

9 Public Law 117-81, Section 559A, 2021.

10 For example, U.S. Code, Title 10, Section 702(c) states that Sections 701, 703, and 704 regarding personnel leave do not apply to academy cadets or midshipmen (U.S. Code, Armed Forces; Subtitle A, General Military Law; Part II, Personnel; Chapter 40, Leave; Section 702, Cadets and Midshipmen; Item C, Inapplicable Leave Provisions).

ance may be needed; and reasons for resignation or disenrollment. DoD and MSA leadership should review reports of this information at least annually, with the goal of improving the policies and practices that support the integration and success of cadet and midshipman parents and the welfare of these parents and their families.

- **DoD should also require the MSAs to collect and analyze data and submit an assessment of the implementation of parental rights–related policy changes on the MSAs' ability to execute their missions and any associated impacts to cadet and midshipman culture, morale, and quality of life.** Reports should be submitted at certain milestones after implementation of the Secretary of Defense's new policy (e.g., the one-, three-, and five-year points) to allow time for the academies to accumulate experience and data regarding implementation and to provide a mechanism for DoD to assess potential impact and any need for additional guidance or policy refinements.

Contents

Tables

CHAPTER 1

Introduction

The U.S. military service academies (MSAs) are four-year bachelor's of science degree–granting institutions and military officer commissioning sources.[1] By law, MSA graduates incur service obligations of at least five years on active duty.[2] The military departments run the MSAs, providing academic curricula, military training, and professional development. The students—known as *cadets* at the U.S. Air Force Academy (USAFA) and the U.S. Military Academy (USMA) and as *midshipmen* at the U.S. Naval Academy (USNA)—must live in dorms on campus and abide by academy regulations, restrictions, and discipline regarding their behavior, appearance, liberty, and physical fitness. Mandatory activities span the calendar year, including summer months. Privileges (e.g., passes to leave campus or permission to have a car at the MSA) are increasingly available as students progress each year.

Cadets and midshipmen may choose from a variety of academic majors, athletic programs, and clubs. Tuition, room, board, certain benefits, and a stipend are fully funded through a congressional authorization and appropriation. The estimated cost per four-year graduate has been reported to be $400,000 to $600,000 in taxpayer dollars.[3] Cadets and midshipmen who voluntarily or involuntary disenroll during the third or fourth year of school may owe the government full or partial repayment of the costs of their education. Graduates are commissioned as military officers and then receive training specific to their occupation (e.g., infantry, pilot, cyberspace operations), as well as continued leadership development. MSA requirements are

[1] Other sources of officer commissions are Reserve Officers' Training Corps (ROTC) associated with baccalaureate programs at civilian colleges and universities, Officer Candidate School/Officer Training School for enlisted personnel or civilians with a bachelor's degree, and direct commissioning of professionals with special expertise (e.g., lawyers, physicians).

[2] For the U.S. Military Academy (USMA), see U.S. Code, Title 10, Armed Forces; Subtitle B, Army; Part III, Training; Chapter 753, United States Military Academy; Section 7448, Cadets: Agreement to Serve as Officer. For the U.S. Naval Academy (USNA), see U.S. Code, Title 10, Armed Forces; Subtitle C, Navy and Marine Corps; Part III, Education and Training; Chapter 853, United States Naval Academy; Section 8459, Midshipmen: Agreement for Length of Service. For the U.S. Air Force Academy (USAFA), see U.S. Code, Title 10, Armed Forces; Subtitle D, Air Force and Space Force; Part III, Training; Chapter 953, United States Air Force Academy; Section 9448, Cadets: Agreement to Serve as Officer.

[3] Kristy N. Kamarck, *Defense Primer: Military Service Academies*, Congressional Research Service, IF11788, December 9, 2021, p. 2.

extremely demanding, but graduates receive a free, high-quality education and guaranteed employment with competitive pay and benefits (including dependent benefits).

Department of Defense Instruction (DoDI) 1322.22, *Service Academies*, includes standardized guidance for all MSAs on their missions and organization; cadets and midshipmen qualifications and eligibility; development and training; management of failure to meet standards, graduate, or complete the service obligation; and graduation and commission requirements.[4] It prohibits cadets and midshipmen at the MSAs from having dependents, clarifying that they cannot have "a legally recognized obligation to provide support" to anyone, including a spouse or child.[5] Cadets or midshipmen who have become parents while enrolled have been required to sever their legal obligation to support the child, resign from the academy, or face involuntary disenrollment. The rationale is that an individual cannot meet both parental and MSA obligations, as this policy excerpt illustrates:

> Pregnancy, being responsible for the pregnancy of another, or being a parent or legal guardian creates significant responsibilities. Such responsibilities are incompatible with the stringent demands placed upon individuals by the Naval Academy's training program and severely interfere with a Midshipman's ability to concentrate full attention and energy to his or her academic, professional, physical, and military duties.[6]

As discussed further in Chapter 3, all the MSAs allow cadets or midshipmen to take a leave of absence to tend to their parental matters and arrange for the relinquishment of their rights, then return to the academies to continue their education and training. Each academy has slightly different approaches to facilitating this arrangement, but all academies have maintained policies and procedures consistent with DoDI 1322.22.

Section 559A of the fiscal year (FY) 2022 National Defense Authorization Act (NDAA) requires a change to this prohibition, directing that

> the Secretary of Defense, after consultation with the Secretaries of the military departments and the Superintendent of each military service academy, shall prescribe regulations that include the option to preserve parental guardianship rights of a cadet or midshipman who becomes pregnant or fathers a child while attending a military service academy, consistent with the individual and academic responsibilities of such cadet or midshipman.[7]

---

4 DoDI 1322.22, *Service Academies*, U.S. Department of Defense, September 24, 2015.

5 DoDI 1322.22, 2015, pp. 10, 21.

6 Commandant of Midshipmen Instruction (COMDTMIDNINST) 1531.2B, *Procedures and Instructions in Cases of Midshipman Pregnancy/Parenthood/Dependency*, U.S. Naval Academy, April 6, 2015, p. 1.

7 Public Law 117-81, National Defense Authorization Act for Fiscal Year 2022, Section 559A, Regulations on Certain Parental Guardianship Rights of Cadets and Midshipmen, December 27, 2021. Although this text says, "parental guardianship rights," *parental rights* and *guardianship rights* are two separate things, as

With this policy change, cadets and midshipmen who become parents may need to continuously manage the competing demands of parenthood and MSA requirements. Policy decisions will have an impact on these parents' ability to meet the needs of their children, succeed at school, and become exemplary military officers. Possible examples of negative military service outcomes include poor academic achievement, poor professional development, failure to graduate, and a quality candidate not commissioning as an officer. Possible examples of negative family outcomes include child abuse and neglect, poor parent-child bonding, poor psychological well-being, financial difficulties (e.g., homeless co-parent and child, food insecurity), legal costs of child support and custody actions, involuntary termination of parental rights, and disenrollment before graduation with heavy education repayment debt.

Research Objective and Scope

Our project's objective was to characterize the legal, policy, practice, and cost implications of changing the U.S. Department of Defense (DoD)'s MSA rules to comply with the directives of the FY 2022 NDAA. The intent of this report is to share our findings and recommendations on changes to support the new policy, some of which could require requests for legislative changes to the new mandate.

The research questions guiding our approach to fulfilling these objectives are as follows:

1. What are the state-level legal responsibilities and requirements of parents that might have implications for cadets and midshipmen and for DoD policies and costs?
2. What DoD regulations, policies, and practices need to be reconsidered or changed to comply with the congressional direction?
3. What DoD regulations, policies, and practices offer examples that could be applied to the MSAs?
4. Are any other congressional legislative changes needed to ensure the parental rights of cadets and midshipmen?
5. What are the potential costs to DoD associated with allowing cadets and midshipmen to maintain their parental rights?

Our scope includes the three DoD MSAs—USAFA, USMA, and USNA—because our research sponsor (the Office of the Under Secretary of Defense for Personnel and Readiness, Manpower and Reserve Affairs) is within the Office of the Secretary of Defense (OSD), and Section 559A of the FY 2022 NDAA focused on OSD.[8] To help prevent gaps in our policy

we will explain in Chapter 2. Thus, throughout this report, we refer to *cadet and midshipman parental rights* (not *guardianship rights*), as is clear from the context of the law.

[8] The NDAA and our research did not focus on the U.S. Coast Guard Academy, operated by the U.S. Coast Guard under the Department of Homeland Security, or the U.S. Merchant Marine Academy, operated by the U.S. Maritime Administration.

review, we were permitted to follow the progress of the concurrent policy review being conducted by OSD's working group on parental rights of cadets and midshipmen. This study was not constrained, however, by any potential course of action discussed within that group. To inform current and potential future deliberations, we sought a comprehensive understanding of the policy and cost implications, including courses of action that may require legislative changes or diverge from DoD's current plans.

Overview of Our Approach

We used multiple approaches and data sources to further understand the potential implications of cadets and midshipmen being allowed to be parents. To address research question 1, we reviewed state laws and statutes and cross-state agreements related to family law, particularly regarding the grounds for termination of parental rights. To address research questions 2–4, we reviewed relevant military-specific U.S. Code and policies and procedures from OSD, the military departments, and the MSAs. We solicited input from senior representatives from OSD, military departments, and MSAs on the relevant policies, regulations, and practices to consider. We briefed our findings and recommendations to senior MSA leaders and staff, including the USMA and USAFA Superintendents and the USNA Commandant and Deputy Commandant, to solicit their feedback prior to finalizing this report. To support our cost analyses to address research question 5, we requested relevant demographic and cost data from OSD, the military departments, and the MSAs. As described in Chapter 4 and Appendix B, because not all of these data existed or were provided, we used publicly available alternatives and varied the potential demographic characteristics in our hypothetical scenarios. These cost analyses relied on the best available data to consider the cost of various policy options to support cadets or midshipmen who are parents.

Future field research could provide additional insights from the perspectives of recent cadets and midshipmen who became parents and from the perspectives of their peers, MSA faculty and staff, and local service providers on the potential implementation challenges, supports that would be helpful, and local needs for policy or other types of guidance or resources.

Organization of the Report

Chapter 2 describes the research approach and findings for the review of the family law context. Our approach to the military-specific federal law and DoD policy review and subsequent findings are provided in Chapter 3 (with methodological search, coding, and analysis details in Appendix A). Chapter 4 summarizes the approach and findings for the cost analyses (with additional cost results presented in Appendix B). Chapter 5 synthesizes what we learned from our research and offers recommendations for structuring military policy changes and supports to help cadet and midshipman parents meet basic parental obligations and succeed as military officers and to assess the implementation and impacts of those changes.

CHAPTER 2

Family Law Context of Parental Rights and Responsibilities

Cadets and midshipmen who become parents must comply with the policies and guidelines of the military. At the same time, they are also subject to broader state and uniform laws surrounding parental rights. To better understand this legal framework and its implications for DoD policy revisions, we reviewed key family law concepts as well as state and uniform laws pertaining to parental rights and responsibilities and alternative caregiving arrangements. The underlying motivation for our legal review is to examine whether DoD policy could end up causing cadets and midshipmen to effectively lose their parental rights, regardless of change in the law, if DoD retains policies that require cadets and midshipmen to live in the dorms, that restrict their ability to leave the academy grounds, and that do not provide any additional pay or benefits to support dependents.

Family law (also known as *domestic relations law*) is an area of legal practice that deals with family-related issues, such as marriage, divorce, child custody, and child support. Family law includes

- state domestic relations laws[1]
- uniform laws and policy (e.g., child support enforcement, interstate custody disputes)
- case law (at the state and federal levels)
- state and federal social and tax laws (e.g., welfare, entitlements such as Social Security benefits).[2]

Historically, family law was governed by state law, with each state legislature determining how to regulate marriage, divorce, support obligations, property rights, and other family matters.[3] These laws were then enforced in state courts. Even though there is variation in

[1] Throughout this report, we use *state* as shorthand to mean the 50 states; the District of Columbia; and the U.S. territories of American Samoa, Guam, the Northern Mariana Islands, Puerto Rico, and the U.S. Virgin Islands.

[2] John E. B. Myers, *Family Law in a Nutshell*, 7th ed., West Publishing, 2019, pp. 3–4.

[3] Linda D. Elrod, "The Federalization of Family Law," *Human Rights Magazine*, Vol. 36, No. 3, Summer 2009.

family law regulations and case law across states, there also are several key family law concepts that the states have in common. The Uniform Law Commission drafts and promotes enactment of uniform state laws, including in family law.[4] States may then adopt these uniform laws. Also, there are federal statutes governing family law. This chapter provides a high-level overview of key concepts and highly relevant state, uniform, and federal laws.

Legal Review Approach

Our research sought to develop a high-level overview of particularly relevant aspects of the family law environment in which cadet and midshipman parents, their children, and other caregivers exercise their rights and responsibilities. We began with more-focused legal review on relevant family law statutes within the three states where the MSAs are located: Colorado (USAFA), Maryland (USNA), and New York (USMA). Our approach focused on key family law concepts and statutes complemented by targeted deep dives on specific topics of particular interest to OSD because of these topics' implications for policy development and the implementation of the FY 2022 NDAA requirements. The central focus of the deep dives was to gain a better understanding of the grounds for involuntary loss of parental rights and, if those right are terminated (either voluntarily or involuntarily), whether the state would permit future reinstatement and how that would occur.

Could the co-parent ask the state court to terminate the cadet's or midshipman's parental rights on the grounds of lack of child support or time spent with the child? If the law requires parents to financially support their children to maintain parental rights, might this indicate the need for other policy changes (e.g., providing an additional stipend) for cadets and midshipmen to meet this obligation? Likewise, cadets and midshipmen have many time-intensive educational, training, and other requirements at the MSAs to balance with their parental obligations. Do the time-intensive MSA requirements alone increase the legal risk for cadet or midshipman parents to involuntarily lose their parental rights? Although our research cannot address every aspect of a cadet's or midshipman's circumstances, our findings can help guide the development and implementation of policies to better support cadet and midshipman parents.

Although family law is predominately state-level law, we found that these questions could largely be answered by reviewing key concepts in family law and a few highly relevant uniform and federal laws related to child support, child custody, and parental rights.[5] A review of

[4] The Uniform Law Commission was established in 1892. It is a nonprofit, unincorporated association with state commissions for each of the 50 states, the District of Columbia, Puerto Rico, and the U.S. Virgin Islands. Its purpose is to "provide states with non-partisan, well-conceived and well-drafted legislation that brings clarity and stability to critical areas of state statutory law." See Uniform Law Commission, "About Us," webpage, undated-a.

[5] To conduct the legal review, we used commercial and academic search engines, such as LexisNexis, Google Scholar, and HeinOnline. We also reviewed state-specific websites, such as those providing the

the common standards across states provides a basis for understanding the legal obligations that cadets and midshipmen may face.

As an example, all states require parents to provide financial support for their children. The states also provide for some form of alternative caregiving arrangements, whether informal or formal, such as kinship care or guardianship. In making decisions about the best living situation and support for a child, the court examines several factors to determine what is in the best interests of the child. In prescribed circumstances, the state can intervene in the family to protect children from harm. If certain conditions are met and there is a compelling justification, a court may involuntarily terminate a parent's rights and responsibilities to their child.

Note that this chapter does not present a comprehensive review of all state laws relating to family law. It is possible that unique circumstances of particular family law cases may require a more detailed review of state law that was beyond the scope of this project.

Key Concepts in Family Law

Cadet and midshipman parents may need to navigate a legal environment of state and federal family laws. Although state laws may vary on the details, they share as their foundation many key concepts, which we describe in this section.

Parental rights broadly refer to "a parent's rights to make all decisions concerning his or her child, including the right to determine the child's care and custody, the right to educate and discipline the child, and the right to control the child's earnings and property."[6] Under constitutional and case law, parents have broad authority to exercise these parental rights over the care, upbringing, and education of their children.[7] These rights include both legal custody and physical custody.

Custody is the "care, control, and maintenance of a child awarded by a court to a responsible adult."[8] Custody has two elements: *legal custody* and *physical custody. Legal custody* refers to a person's legal decisionmaking responsibility, which is defined as "the authority to make significant decisions on a child's behalf, including decisions about education, religious training, and healthcare."[9] *Physical custody*, also known as *residential custody*, refers to "the right to have

---

state's legal codes and other court and informational resources for parents, caregivers, and family law practitioners. Examples of search terms used for databases include "child support obligation," "guardian," "kinship care," "failure to support," "termination of parental rights," "involuntary termination of parental rights," and "military parent." Among the search results, we reviewed primary (e.g., state statutes) and secondary (e.g., legal primers, law review articles) sources.

[6] Bryan A. Garner, ed., *A Handbook of Family Law Terms*, West Group, 2001, p. 428.

[7] See, e.g., Myers, 2019, p. 7.

[8] Garner, 2001, p. 151.

[9] Garner, 2001, p. 161.

the child live with the person awarded custody by the court" and "possession of a child during visitation."[10] Although a person need not have both physical and legal custody over the child, they often occur in tandem. Alternative caregiving arrangements, such as *kinship care* or *guardianship* (discussed later in this section), may involve legal custody, physical custody, or both.

Just as parents have rights, they also have legal obligations. According to a widely used legal reference, *A Handbook of Family Law Terms*, these obligations can be grouped into parenting functions, which are "tasks that serve the direct or day-to-day needs of a child or of a child's family. Parenting functions include providing economic support, making decisions about the child's welfare, maintaining the family residence and the family vehicle, and buying food and clothes."[11] A key parenting function is provision of child support, which is "a parent's legal obligation to contribute to the economic maintenance and education of a child until the age of majority, the child's emancipation before reaching majority, or the child's completion of secondary education."[12] Child support can be enforced both civilly (e.g., contempt of court; wage garnishment) and criminally (e.g., possible incarceration). It is important to note that child support is the right of the child, not of the person caring for the child.[13] Each state has a child support obligation, although there may be differences in how a parent's obligation is calculated.[14]

It is not realistic for every child to live with a parent. Therefore, states provide for alternative arrangements,[15] such as kinship care or guardianship of the child. *Kinship care* refers to "the care of children by relatives, or in some jurisdictions, close family friends (often referred to as fictive kin)."[16] Kinship care can be either an informal arrangement or formally established by a court, whereas *guardianship* is a formal caregiving arrangement. A guardian is defined as "one who has the legal authority and duty to care for another's person or property, especially because of another's infancy, incapacity, or disability. A guardian may be appointed either for all purposes or a specific purpose."[17]

The federal Children's Bureau describes guardianship as "most frequently used when relative caregivers wish to provide a permanent home for the child and maintain the child's family

[10] Garner, 2001, p. 163.

[11] Garner, 2001, p. 430.

[12] Garner, 2001, p. 102.

[13] Garner, 2001, p. 102

[14] Each state has a method for calculating a person's child support obligation. These methods include the income shares model, the percentage of income model, and the Melson formula. Where appropriate, a court may deviate from the statutory child support guidelines.

[15] Although states provide for some form of these caregiving arrangements, the names for and specific details and processes of each may vary.

[16] Child Welfare Information Gateway, "Kinship Care," webpage, undated-b.

[17] Garner, 2001, p. 278.

members without a termination of parental rights, as is required for adoption."[18] Guardianship is established by the court. Kinship care and guardianship do not require a caregiver to have all the rights and responsibilities of a parent. They also do not require the legal severing of a parent's relationship with the child. For example, a parent may maintain legal custody of their child and exercise visitation, although the child resides with a relative who provides for the child's day-to-day needs.

Federal law requires that within 30 days after a child has been removed from parental custody, the state must identify and provide notice to all grandparents and other adult relatives of the child. However, support and rights granted to kinship caregivers varies by state. Some states allow kinship caregivers rights to medical and educational consent over the child without having to obtain legal custody. Many states use Title IV-E funds to grant guardianship assistance payments to kinship caregivers.[19]

When the court is involved in custodial decisionmaking, it uses some form of the *best interests of the child standard.* Despite its name, there is no uniform "standard." Instead, this term refers to the case-by-case deliberative process that a court uses in determining the arrangement and support that would best benefit the child.[20] State statutes vary in referencing guideline principles of the best interests of the child and the factors that a court should consider in making such a determination. That said, there are some common factors:

- the emotional ties and relationships between a child and their parents, siblings, family, household members, and/or other caregivers
- the parent's capacity to provide a safe home, adequate food, clothing, and medical care and to meet the child's basic needs
- the mental and physical needs of the child
- the mental and physical health of the parents
- domestic violence in the home or other criminal activity
- the child's age and wishes (depending on state and age).[21]

Some states also identify factors that may not be considered in a court's "best interests of the child" deliberation. As described by the Children's Bureau, some states prevent consideration

[18] Child Welfare Information Gateway, "Guardianship," webpage, undated-a.

[19] *Title IV-E funding* refers to Title IV-E of the Social Security Act (U.S. Code, Title 42, The Public Health and Welfare; Chapter 7, Social Security; Subchapter IV, Grant to State for Aid and Services to Needy Families with Children for Child Welfare Services; Part E, Federal Payments for Foster Care, Prevention, and Permanency). Title IV-E funding includes an optional formula grant to states and tribal entities that provides guardianship assistance payments for the care of children by relatives who have assumed legal guardianship.

[20] Garner, 2001, p. 77.

[21] Child Welfare Information Gateway, *Determining the Best Interests of the Child*, U.S. Department of Health and Human Services, Administration for Children and Families, Children's Bureau, 2020.

of the socioeconomic status, sex, gender, or disability of a parent or caregiver.[22] States may also assert that a court should not weigh any one factor more than another in making its decision.

In certain circumstances, the state may intervene in the family relationship to ensure the safety, care, and well-being of the child. *Termination of parental rights (TPR)* refers to "the legal severing of a parent's rights, privileges, and responsibilities regarding his or her child."[23] TPR is a severe intervention that requires many steps, extensive evidence, and layers of review and protection; it is referred to colloquially as family law's "death penalty."[24] TPR can be voluntary or involuntary, and it is a decision made after careful deliberation. Before involuntarily terminating parental rights, many states require a court to "determine, by clear and convincing evidence, that the parent is unfit" and to "determine whether severing the parent-child relationship is in the child's best interests."[25] We discuss TPR further in the rest of this chapter.

Federal and Uniform Laws

In addition to family law concepts, the following key federal and uniform laws are most relevant: legal protections for service members, cross-state child custody agreements, and cross-state child support agreements.

Servicemembers Civil Relief Act

The Servicemembers Civil Relief Act (SCRA)[26] was enacted in 2003 as a revision and expansion of the Soldiers' and Sailors' Civil Relief Act of 1940, which aimed to ease financial burdens on active-duty service members during periods of military service.[27] SCRA's purpose is to "provide for the temporary suspension of judicial and administrative proceedings and transactions that may adversely affect the civil rights of service members during their military service."[28] SCRA applies to all military services,[29] and it includes cadets and midship-

[22] Child Welfare Information Gateway, 2020.

[23] Garner, 2001.

[24] See William Vesneski, "State Law and the Termination of Parental Rights," *Family Court Review*, Vol. 49, No. 2, April 2011, p. 364.

[25] Child Welfare Information Gateway, *Grounds for Involuntary Termination of Parental Rights: Determining the Best Interests of the Child*, U.S. Department of Health and Human Services, Administration for Children and Families, Children's Bureau, 2021, p. 2.

[26] U.S. Code, Title 50, War and National Defense; Chapter 50, Servicemembers Civil Relief; Sections 3901–4043.

[27] U.S. Department of Justice, "Servicemembers Civil Relief Act Summary," webpage, December 13, 2021.

[28] U.S. Code, Title 50, Section 3902, Purpose.

[29] SCRA uses the "armed forces" and "uniformed services" definitions contained in Section 101 of U.S. Code, Title 10, which applies to members of the U.S. Army, Navy, Air Force, Marine Corps, and Coast Guard (U.S. Code, Title 10, Armed Forces; Subtitle A, General Military Law; Part I, Organization and Gen-

men in the definition of "servicemembers."[30] SCRA provides the following service member protections in child custody actions:

- stay against default judgments when the defendant service member does not make an appearance[31]
- stay against civil proceedings if current military duties or lack of military authorization prevent the service member from appearing in court[32]
- stay or vacation of execution of court judgments, attachments, and garnishments if military service limits the service member's ability to comply[33]
- temporary custodial responsibilities based solely on a service member's anticipated or actual deployment that may only last for the period of deployment[34]
- for actions seeking permanent modification of custody, prevents a court from considering a service member's anticipated or actual deployment as the sole factor in its determination of the best interests of the child[35]
- ensures that, in cases in which state law provides greater protections to the service member than SCRA, those greater protections apply[36]
- requires services to provide notice of SCRA's child custody protections to service members annually and before each deployment.[37]

Thus, the SCRA may afford cadets and midshipmen some protection from lawsuits by their co-parents (or others) for custody or financial support. However, these cadets and midshipmen could still incur significant legal expenses for family court matters.

---

eral Military Powers; Chapter 1, Definitions, Rules of Construction, Cross References, and Related Matters; Section 101, Definitions).

30 Relevant to cadets and midshipmen, SCRA defines "military service" as including the "active duty" definition in Section 101(d) of U.S. Code, Title 10: "Such term includes full-time training duty, annual training duty, and attendance, while in the active military service, at a school designated as a service school by law or by the Secretary of the military department concerned. Such term does not include full-time National Guard duty." This definition does not include cadets or midshipmen who are not on active-duty status (e.g., those who are on administrative leave). See U.S. Code, Title 10, Section 101, Subpart d, Duty Status.

31 U.S. Code, Title 50, Section 3931, Protection of Servicemembers Against Default Judgment.

32 U.S. Code, Title 50, Section 3932, Stay of Proceedings When Servicemember Has Notice.

33 U.S. Code, Title 50, Section 3934, Stay or Vacation of Execution of Judgments, Attachments, and Garnishments.

34 U.S. Code, Title 50, Section 3938, Child Custody Protection; Subpart a, Duration of Temporary Custody Order Based on Certain Deployment.

35 U.S. Code, Title 50, Section 3938, Subpart b, Limitation on Consideration of Member's Deployment in Determination of Child's Best Interest.

36 U.S. Code, Title 50, Section 3938, Subpart d, Preemption.

37 U.S. Code, Title 50, Section 3938a, Annual Notice to Members of the Armed Forces Regarding Child Custody Protections Guaranteed by the Servicemembers Civil Relief Act.

Full Faith and Credit for Child Support Orders

The Full Faith and Credit for Child Support Orders Act of 1994 was enacted to require a state to recognize and enforce child support orders from sister states until the state no longer has continuous, exclusive jurisdiction over the matter, the parties, and the child.[38] The purpose of the law was to prevent *forum shopping*, a colloquial term in the legal profession whereby litigants search for courts they believe would be more favorable to their case, no matter how tenuous the court's connection to the case or the parties. Under the statutory language, "continuous, exclusive jurisdiction" over the initial child support exists unless (1) the new state has subject-matter jurisdiction over the matter (i.e., family court of the new state); (2) the new state has personal jurisdiction over the parties because neither party nor the child reside in the original state; and (3) the parties receive reasonable notice and opportunity to be heard in the modification case.[39] In the Personal Responsibility and Work Opportunity Reconciliation Act of 1996, Congress amended the Full Faith and Credit for Child Support Orders Act so its provisions are consistent with those in the Uniform Interstate Family Support Act (UIFSA).[40]

Uniform Interstate Family Support Act

UIFSA allows enforcement of child support orders issued by an out-of-state court.[41] UIFSA was first developed in 1992 and has undergone multiple revisions since. It provides for both intrastate and international enforcement of U.S. child support orders, "ensur[ing] that children residing in the United States will receive the financial support due from parents, wherever the parents reside."[42] It also provides registration, recognition, enforcement, and modification of foreign support orders from countries that are parties to the Hague Convention. It has been enacted by all 50 states, the District of Columbia, Puerto Rico, and the U.S. Virgin Islands.[43]

---

[38] Public Law 103-383, Full Faith and Credit for Child Support Orders Act; Section 3, Full Faith and Credit for Child Support Orders; Part a, In General, October 20, 1994.

[39] Public Law 103-383, 1994.

[40] Office of Child Support Enforcement, *Applicability of the Full Faith and Credit for Child Support Orders Act to States and Tribes*, Action Transmittal 02-03, May 28, 2002, current as of September 24, 2021.

[41] Uniform Law Commission, "Interstate Family Support Act," webpage, undated-c.

[42] Uniform Law Commission, undated-c.

[43] The Preventing Sex Trafficking and Strengthening Families Act of 2014 required each state to implement the 2008 UIFSA amendments (regarding international enforcement of U.S. child support orders and vice versa) as a condition of receiving federal fundings for state child support enforcement organizations. See Public Law 113-183, Preventing Sex Trafficking and Strengthening Families Act of 2014, September 29, 2014; and Uniform Law Commission, undated-c.

Uniform Child Custody Jurisdiction and Enforcement Act

The 1997 Uniform Child Custody Jurisdiction and Enforcement Act (UCCJEA) is a uniform act limiting state jurisdiction over child custody to avoid competing orders.[44] It also provides for a jurisdiction's enforcement of child custody orders from a sister jurisdiction. Generally, a state defers to the child's home state court in a custody matter. That state will maintain continuous, exclusive jurisdiction unless certain criteria are met, such as the parents and child no longer live in the home state. The state can exercise temporary emergency jurisdiction to protect safety until the case is transferred to the home state. As of October 2022, the UCCJEA has been adopted by 49 states (the exception is Massachusetts), the District of Columbia, Guam, Puerto Rico, and the U.S. Virgin Islands.

Potential Risk of Involuntary Termination of Parental Rights at MSAs

Cadets and midshipmen maintain a rigorous schedule of physical and academic training, with little personal free time and short school breaks. Raising a child also requires significant time and financial support. This tension between cadet and midshipman responsibilities and parental obligations could put cadets and midshipmen who become parents at risk of involuntary TPR. We conducted a deeper legal review into the grounds and processes for involuntary TPR to assess this potential risk.

Grounds for Termination of Parental Rights

The Adoption and Safe Families Act of 1997 (ASFA) establishes eight grounds for involuntary TPR.[45] In his review of ASFA and state TPR criteria, William Vesneski divided the ASFA criteria into two categories (see Table 2.1):

- *fast-track* criteria, under which the state is not required to first undertake reasonable efforts to reunify the parent and child before filing for involuntary TPR
- TPR for children in foster care for a certain duration.[46]

There is variation across states in terms of both the circumstances in which a court may involuntarily terminate a parent's rights and whether parental rights can be reinstated after a termination. A 2020 assessment by the National Conference of State Legislatures found that "[a]pproximately 22 states have legislation in place that allows for the reinstatement of paren-

[44] Uniform Law Commission, "Child Custody Jurisdiction and Enforcement Act" webpage, undated-b.

[45] Public Law 105-89, Adoption and Safe Families Act of 1997, November 19, 1997.

[46] Vesneski, 2011.

TABLE 2.1
ASFA Criteria for Fast-Tracking Involuntary TPR

ASFA Criteria	Fast-Track?
Abandonment of the child (as defined by relevant state statute)	Yes
Torture of the child	Yes
Chronic abuse of the child	Yes
Sexual abuse of the child	Yes
Murder or voluntary manslaughter of another child of the parent[a]	Yes
Felony assault of the child or another child of the parent resulting in serious bodily injury	Yes
Termination of parental rights of another child of the parent	Yes
Child in foster care for 15 of the previous 22 months	No

SOURCE: Features information from Vesneski, 2011, pp. 364, 367.

[a] ASFA criteria apply to both commission of murder/voluntary manslaughter and aiding, abetting, attempting, conspiring, or soliciting such murder. See Public Law 105-89, Title I, Reasonable Efforts and Safety Requirements for Foster Care and Adoption Placements; Section 101, Clarification of the Reasonable Efforts Requirement, January 7, 1997.

tal rights."[47] Many state statutes include additional criteria for involuntary TPR. Table 2.2 shows common grounds for TPR. We note that an in-depth survey of all state laws regarding TPR is beyond the scope of this effort; we also note that judges consider the unique circumstances of each case, so the information provided in this report cannot capture every basis for which involuntary TPR has occurred.

As demonstrated in Table 2.2, involuntary TPR grounds are a mix of more-measurable or well-defined grounds (e.g., born exposed to alcohol and/or drugs, child abuse) and more-subjective grounds (e.g., abandonment of a child). The more-subjective grounds leave room for interpretation by a judge, making it difficult to definitively determine what actions (or lack of actions) would be considered, for instance, abandonment of the child, failure to maintain contact with the child, or failure to support the child. A strict interpretation of these grounds could put a cadet or midshipman parent at risk of involuntary TPR if they are unable to regularly visit the child or provide significant financial support.

However, barring additional factors (e.g., meeting one of the other involuntary TPR grounds), our review suggests it is unlikely that a parent would be subject to involuntary TPR based solely on the constraints imposed by the MSAs. For example, grounds including abandonment of a child, failure to support the child, and failure to maintain contact with the child often require the actions to occur for a statutorily set period.[48]

[47] National Conference of State Legislatures, "Reinstatement of Parental Rights State Statute Summary," January 17, 2020.

[48] For example,

> a court may find that good cause exists for termination of parental rights for a parent who . . . has been determined by clear and convincing evidence to have subjected the child or another child . . . abandonment for at least six months . . . (South Dakota Codified Laws, Title 26, Minors; Chapter 26-8A, Protection of Children from Abuse or Neglect; Section 26-8A.1, Termination of Parental Rights—Good Cause Considerations, 2022).

TABLE 2.2
Common Involuntary TPR Criteria Across States

Category Description	TPR Criteria
Child abuse and neglect	• Born exposed to drugs/alcohol • Chronic abuse and/or neglect • Emotional/mental abuse of the child • Serious bodily injury to child • Sexual abuse • Torture
Parental fitness	• Abandonment of child • Child conceived as a result of rape • Criminal convictions (depends on nature of crime) • Domestic violence • Failure to establish paternity • Failure to respond to/comply with reasonable efforts by social workers/court • Involuntary TPR of another child • Murder/manslaughter of other parent or child's sibling • Parental incarceration/institutionalization • Parental mental illness or incompetency • Parental substance abuse (chronic) • Prior involvement with child welfare • Willful, extended failure to maintain contact with the child • Willful, extended failure to support the child

SOURCES: Features information from Child Welfare Information Gateway, 2021; Public Law 105-89; Alan D. Scheinkman and Matthew W. Lisle, "Child Custody and Visitation," Section 28.02, Elements of the Proceeding, *Child Custody and Visitation Law and Practice*, Matthew Bender & Co., Release 77, October 2022; and Vesneski, 2011.

Additionally, state statutes often include language requiring some degree of "willfulness" or lack of "good cause" to meet these TPR grounds.[49] Reviews of state TPR statutes and language

[49] For example,

> the juvenile court may upon petition, terminate all rights of a parent to a child . . . if it finds that one of more of the following conditions exist . . . that a parent has been ordered to contribute to the support of the child or financially aid in the child's birth and has continuously failed to do so without good cause. This clause shall not be construed to state a grounds for termination of parental rights of a noncustodial parent if that parent has not been ordered to or cannot financially contribute to the support of the child or aid in a child's birth. (Minnesota Statutes, Chapter 260C, Child Protection, Section 260C.301, Termination of Parental Rights, 2022)

> The court may terminate parental rights . . . when the court finds such action to be in the best interests of the juvenile and it appears by the evidence that one or more of the following conditions exist: (1) the parents have abandoned the juvenile for six months or more immediately prior to the filing of the petition . . . (3) the parents, being financially able, have willfully neglected to provide the juvenile with the necessary subsistence, education, or other care necessary for his or her health, morals, or welfare or have neglected to pay for such subsistence, education, or other care when legal custody of the juvenile is lodged with others and such payment ordered by the court.(Revised Statutes of Nebraska, Chapter 43, Infants and Juveniles; Article 2, Juvenile Code; Section 43-292, Termination of Parental Rights; Grounds, 2022)

> [T]he court may find abandonment of the child if a parent or guardian has shown a conscious disregard of parental responsibilities toward the child by failing to provide reasonable support, maintain regular contact, or provide normal supervision . . . . Abandonment also includes instances when the parent or guardian, without justifiable cause, (1) left the child with another person without provision for the child's support and without meaningful communication with the child for a period of three months; (2) has

discussing best interests of the child demonstrate that parental fitness includes the *quality* of the relationship and care, not just some quantitative metric. For example, parents may communicate with their child in person, over the phone, by mail, or by electronic means (such as video chat or email). Parents may use a mix of these communication methods with varying frequency.

A person's child support obligation is determined using set computational guidelines assessing factors that include the parents' gross income, time with the child, and other allowable expenses (e.g., housing, child care). Using these income, cost, and other factors, child support is calculated based on a sliding scale. Mechanisms addressing failure to pay child support are enforced by the federal, state, and local-cooperative Title IV-D program overseen by the Federal Office of Child Support Enforcement. These mechanisms can include the suspension of a driver's license or passport, revocation of professional or occupational licenses, or immediate income withholding. Immediate income withholding, the garnishment of a noncustodial parent's wages for child support, is not automatic and occurs only after a court order of support is issued. Immediate income withholding can either be requested voluntarily by the noncustodial parent or be ordered because of nonpayment.

Even with set guidelines, courts are permitted to deviate from the child support guidelines when necessary. Along with the court order of support, a judge may issue a "good cause" exemption that allows for an exemption from immediate income withholding. Federal regulation states that a "good cause" finding must be based on either (1) a written determination of why immediate wage withholding would not be in the best interests of the child or (2) the proof of timely payment of support in previously issued orders.

Process for Termination of Parental Rights

Involuntary termination of parental rights involves lengthy and contested court processes. Whether an individual, rather than solely the county or state child welfare agency or other governmental entity, can petition for termination of rights varies by state.

As with the grounds for TPR, the TPR process also includes protections and checkpoints for parents and children before courts can order involuntary termination of a parent's rights to the child. In this way, the TPR process reflects the seriousness of the potential outcome.

As with TPR grounds, state statutes provide details on the legal process and procedures in a particular state. However, they follow a similar track across the states. Section 28.02 of *Child Custody and Visitation Law and Practice* provides the following overview of involuntary TPR proceedings:

> In termination proceedings, the petitioner must establish that the local statutory criteria for terminating parental rights has been satisfied. These criteria vary from jurisdiction

made only minimal efforts to communicate with the child; (3) failed for a period of at least six months to maintain regular visitation with the child. (Alaska Statutes, Title 47, Welfare, Social Services, and Institutions; Chapter 10, Children in Need of Aid; Article 1, Children's Proceedings; Section 47.10.013, Abandonment, 2022)

> to jurisdiction. In some jurisdictions, a termination proceeding may be maintained only where an authorized agency has had custody of the child and has been unable to revive or maintain a viable relationship between the natural parent and the child, due to the conduct of the natural parent. In other jurisdictions, the proceeding is not dependent upon prior agency involvement with the child and the focus is more directly focused upon parental conduct which is claimed to be injurious to the child. Note, however, that each and every statutory factor does not have to exist before a court may terminate parental rights. In fact, in some states, the court may make its decision based on the existence of only one factor. In each of these types of statutory schemes, there are due process limitations on the grounds that may be utilized as a predicate for terminating parental rights. Standing to maintain the proceeding is, in large measure, dependent upon the type of proceeding sanctioned in the particular jurisdiction. However, it is fundamental in all jurisdictions that the natural parents be made parties to the proceeding.[50]

Although involuntary TPR considers the best interests of the child, the petitioner also must prove by clear and convincing evidence that at least one of the statutory TPR grounds is met.[51] The burden of proof is on the petitioner to demonstrate that the parent is unfit and parental rights should be terminated.

In states that permit only an authorized state agency (e.g., Division of Youth and Family Services) to initiate the petition, the process begins with removal of the child from the home and an investigation into the alleged concerns (e.g., child abuse or neglect). Except in limited circumstances (see the previous ASFA discussion), the state agency is required to make reasonable efforts to strengthen and reunify the family before it can initiate TPR proceedings.[52] Services provided may include parenting classes, substance abuse treatments, vocational programs, and other steps within the agency's permanency and reunification plan for the family. These steps often have set periods during which a parent may avail themselves of these services, and willful refusal to participate further supports involuntary TPR.

Involuntary TPR proceedings have additional safeguards for the parents. For example, a parent would be served with notice of the proceedings and charges against them. Parents have a right to counsel (although not all states provide counsel for indigent parents), and the child in question is frequently represented by a separate attorney or representative (e.g., Guardian ad litem or a Court-Appointed Special Advocate). Some states permit prehearing discovery of relevant items, such as agency or official records.[53] These proceedings often take place over a period of weeks or months, granting a parent opportunities to learn of and pre-

[50] Scheinkman and Lisle, 2022.

[51] Clear and convincing evidence is a medium-level burden of proof (above preponderance of evidence; below beyond a reasonable doubt). Clear and convincing evidence requires that the evidence is "highly and substantially more likely to be true than untrue" (Wex database, "Clear and Convincing Evidence," Legal Information Institute, undated).

[52] Scheinkman and Lisle, 2022.

[53] Scheinkman and Lisle, 2022.

pare for potential TPR proceedings, participate in them, and try to remediate concerns before an involuntary TPR is ordered.

Key Findings and Conclusions

In this chapter, we provide an overview of key family law concepts and statutes that apply broadly to cadets and midshipmen who become parents. Each state has various statutes, case law, and principles that govern its regulation and oversight of, and intervention in, families. Although state laws and individual court cases vary, they share a foundation in similar family law principles, standards, or practices. Likewise, although family law remains a largely state-driven area, key federal and uniform laws also apply. Our findings from a review of relevant areas of family law highlight how these laws might affect cadets and midshipmen who become parents while at the MSAs.

Parents Do Not Have to Relinquish Parental Rights to Set Up Informal or Formal Alternative Caregiving Arrangements for Their Children

Irrespective of the state with jurisdiction, family law provisions govern the exercise of a cadet's or midshipman's parental rights. Those parental rights include physical custody (e.g., where the child resides) and legal custody (e.g., broad decisionmaking authority over the child). These rights also include responsibilities, such as the requirement to provide financial child support for the care and maintenance of the child. In the event that a parent is unable or unwilling to care for a child, a state will provide for some form of alternative caregiving arrangements for a child.

Although names and details may vary by state, a kinship caregiver relative may house the child and provide for daily needs while the parent maintains broad decisionmaking authority over the child, provides for support, and maintains contact. A state court may appoint a guardian who will handle the physical and financial needs of the child. A child may be removed from the home and placed in foster care. These different arrangements do not require the full suite of parental rights and responsibilities to be transferred to the caregiver; depending on the circumstances, the parent may maintain parental rights while the child resides with someone else on a temporary basis. Arrangements also do not all require formal court proceedings; some may involve informal agreements between private parties.

If a court is involved in the family arrangement, the standard of the best interests of the child will inform the court's decision on the appropriate custodial and care arrangements for the child. In cases in which a state must intervene in the family to pursue involuntary TPR, the court also will consider the best interests of the child and required statutory factors.

Uniform Laws Provide Consistent Standards for Child Custody and Support, and the SCRA Provides Protections for Cadets and Midshipmen

At the national level, a cadet or midshipman parent is subject to such laws as the UCCJEA and UIFSA. These uniform laws have been broadly adopted by states, and they govern family aspects such as jurisdiction over and enforcement of court orders from another state or international location. Cadets and midshipmen also qualify for SCRA protections. These protections permit temporary suspension of judicial actions, including family law matters, for service members during periods of active-duty military service. The SCRA also contains child custody–specific protections, such as permitting temporary custody changes only for the duration of a service member's deployment and forbidding courts from considering deployment as the sole factor in making custodial decisions.

Limited Contact and Financial Support While at the MSAs Would Not Alone Likely Result in Involuntary TPR for Cadet and Midshipman Parents

Because of the unique requirements of an MSA course of study, we also conducted a deeper examination of involuntary termination of a person's parental rights. Specifically, could such constraints as limited time and support negatively affect a cadet's or midshipman's parental rights to the point of having them terminated? Our legal review suggests that, absent other aggravating factors, issues such as limited contact or child support alone likely would not give rise to involuntary TPR for a cadet or midshipman parent. Each state has statutes providing its principles, grounds, and/or processes for involuntarily terminating someone's parental rights. These grounds include a mix of more-straightforward factors (e.g., child abuse, born addicted to drugs or alcohol) and more-ambiguous ones (e.g., failure to support a child, abandonment).

Although the more-ambiguous factors seem like they could apply to a cadet or midshipman parent, a comprehensive consideration of the family circumstances would make this unlikely. State statutes and case law often require these parental "failures" to exist for a set period and to be done willfully or without good cause. For example, a parent must choose not to have any contact with a child for one year for it to be considered abandonment. A parent must willfully refuse to provide any or sufficient child support for their child without good cause for doing so.

Our examination of state statutes and secondary sources demonstrates that courts assess the quality of a parent's relationship with and care for the child, rather than meeting some quantitative metric. Although an MSA may impose unique, temporary constraints on a parent's ability to exercise their parental rights, these constraints alone do not imperil a parent's legal rights and responsibilities for their child. The courts will broadly assess not just *what* a parent is or is not doing but also *why* they are doing it.

We note that our findings cannot guarantee that a cadet or midshipman parent faces no legal risk, only that such risk is minimal if based solely on the limitations imposed by the requirements of an MSA. State statutes vary in the criteria they set for TPR consideration, how explicit or ambiguous those criteria are, and the possibilities for reinstatement. However, SCRA and the guardrails in TPR processes also provide procedural protections for cadet and midshipman parents.

CHAPTER 3

Military Policy Landscape

This chapter describes the changes required by Section 559A of the FY 2022 NDAA and how DoDI 1322.22, the primary DoD policy governing the service academies, must be changed to comply. We then further consider the implications for the U.S. Code and for policies in OSD, the military departments, and local MSAs. DoD's policy decisions could also enhance the ability of cadet and midshipman parents to meet the needs of their children, succeed at school, and become exemplary military officers. Some of the policy options have cost implications, which we discuss further in Chapter 4.

Military Policy Review Approach

In addition to state and uniform family laws discussed in Chapter 2, we conducted a review of relevant military-specific laws, regulations, policies, and practices, which (for brevity's sake) we will refer to collectively as *policies*. Such a review is necessary because changes to one DoD policy can have implications for others. Military department and MSA policies must align with DoD policies and U.S. Code. To avoid contradictory guidance, new or revised policy needs to be consistent with existing policies, or those other policies also need to be updated.

Therefore, to consider the policy implications of the FY 2022 NDAA, we searched for and reviewed relevant policies across the following hierarchical levels: U.S. Code, DoD, military department (i.e., Department of the Air Force, Department of the Army, Department of the Navy) and local MSA. The search included policies for other active-duty personnel and for ROTC cadets and midshipmen that could serve as examples for possible revisions to policies for cadets and midshipmen at the MSAs. Appendix A provides more information about how we searched for, coded, and analyzed the policies.

The FY 2022 NDAA Requirement

Section 559A of the FY 2022 NDAA directs the Secretary of Defense to change DoD policy as follows:

> (a) REGULATIONS REQUIRED.—Not later than one year after the date of the enactment of this Act, Secretary of Defense, after consultation with the Secretaries of the

> military departments and the Superintendent of each military service academy, shall prescribe regulations that include the option to preserve parental guardianship rights of a cadet or midshipman who becomes pregnant or fathers a child while attending a military service academy, consistent with the individual and academic responsibilities of such cadet or midshipman.[1]

The language refers specifically to biological parenthood ("becomes pregnant or fathers a child"), not the social roles of caring for and raising children, which would also include stepparents, adoptive parents, foster parents, and kinship and guardian caregivers. Section 559A also refers to the pregnancy or fathering a child as occurring *while the cadet or midshipman is attending the MSA*. Section 559A further specifies, "Nothing in this section shall be construed to change, or require a change to, any admission requirement at a military service academy."[2] Thus, Congress did not require that parents be allowed to enroll in the MSAs, but Congress also did not expressly prohibit the Secretary of Defense from making that change. It is also notable that, without providing further detail, Section 559A directs that the regulations with the option for cadets and midshipmen to preserve their parental rights be "consistent with the individual and academic responsibilities of such cadet or midshipman." That clause leaves room for interpretation, while supporting the importance of meeting expectations for successful officer development and MSA graduation.

Insights into policy options that Congress considered can be found in the House of Representatives draft language preceding Section 559A.[3] That draft, which was sent to the Senate, was much more prescriptive, with details that did not appear in the legislation.[4] For example, the draft language required that cadets and midshipmen who become parents while enrolled

- must develop a formal family care plan
- must live in the dorms as any other student would
- may not rely on MSA child care facilities
- may not receive any additional pay, leave, or liberty because of having a child
- may not be excused from MSA-required travel, classes, training, or physical fitness requirements because of having a child.

[1] Public Law 117-81, Section 559A, 2021.

[2] Public Law 117-81, Section 559A, 2021.

[3] U.S. House of Representatives, National Defense Authorization Act for Fiscal Year 2022, Bill 4350, Section 559D, Requirement to Issue Regulations Ensuring Certain Parental Guardianship Rights of Cadets and Midshipmen, October 18, 2021.

[4] U.S. House of Representatives, 2021.

The draft legislation also would have allowed cadets and midshipmen fathering a child a leave of absence of at least one week to attend their child's birth.[5] Notably, the House proposed four options for cadet and midshipman parents:

- Take up to a one-year leave of absence from the MSA.
- Seek transfer to an ROTC unit and civilian university.
- Receive a "full release from the covered service academy and any related obligations."
- Enlist as an active-duty service member.[6]

As we learned during this project, it would be far less costly for the government to provide an additional stipend (approximately $15,000) and child care subsidy (approximately $20,000) for one year (which the draft legislation would have prohibited) than it would be to release a parent from service and repayment of one year of their MSA education costs (approximately $91,000, which the draft legislation would have allowed). (For more on this, see Table 4.2 in Chapter 4.) Moreover, if the parent chooses the full release option, the military department loses that talent from its pipeline.

Ultimately, after deliberations, Congress passed the pared-down Section 559A, which directed the Secretary of Defense to develop the regulations.

DoD Policies

As represented by the examples in Table 3.1, DoDI 1322.22 and other policies within the military departments govern the MSAs. Additionally, most of the policies defer decisions on final actions to either academy leadership or the secretary of the military department concerned.

The most obvious policy change needed to comply with the FY 2022 NDAA is a revision of the prohibition of dependents stated in DoDI 1322.22 and echoed in subordinate policies (Department of the Air Force Instruction [DAFI] 36-3501 and Army Regulation [AR] 150-1).[7] Some policies in the Department of the Air Force (e.g., DAFI 36-3501) have already been revised in anticipation of the NDAA requirement. However, the potential downstream policy implications could be much wider. MSA cadets and midshipmen are not typical college students. Their lives are highly structured, and there are great demands on their time, such that policies have outright stated, "It is recognized that the rigors of the Academic, Military, and Physical Programs in the cadet environment are incompatible

---

5 U.S. House of Representatives, 2021.

6 U.S. House of Representatives, 2021.

7 DoDI 1322.22, 2015; DAFI 36-3501, *United States Air Force Academy Operations*, Department of the Air Force, May 9, 2022; AR 150-1, *United States Military Academy: Organization, Administration and Operation*, Department of the Army, January 12, 2021.

TABLE 3.1
Key DoD Policies Governing MSAs with Content Relevant for Revising Parental Rights Policies

Department	Policy
U.S. Department of Defense	DoDI 1322.22, *Service Academies*, U.S. Department of Defense, September 24, 2015
Department of the Air Force	DAFI 36-3501, *United States Air Force Academy Operations*, Department of the Air Force, May 9, 2022
	U.S. Air Force Academy Instruction (USAFAI) 36-2005, *Readmission of Former USAF Academy Cadets*, U.S. Air Force Academy, October 27, 2017, certified current May 27, 2021
	USAFAI 36-2007, *Application for and Administration of Cadet Turnback Program*, U.S. Air Force Academy, April 18, 2007, certified current December 9, 2020
	USAFAI 36-3504, *Disenrollment of United States Air Force Academy Cadets*, U.S. Air Force Academy, August 15, 2022
Department of the Army	AR 150-1, *United States Military Academy: Organization, Administration, and Operation*, Department of the Army, January 12, 2021
	U.S. Commandant of Cadets Policy Memorandum Number CC-20-12, *Procedures and Instructions in Cases of Cadet Pregnancies*, United States Military Academy, November 19, 2020
Department of the Navy	Secretary of the Navy Instruction (SECNAVINST) 1531.2D, *United States Naval Academy Curriculum and Admissions Policy*, Department of the Navy, November 27, 2018
	SECNAVINST1531.4A, *U.S. Naval Academy Midshipmen Disenrollment*, Department of the Navy, November 28, 2018
	COMDTMIDNINST 1531.2B, *Procedures and Instructions in Cases of Midshipman Pregnancy/Parenthood/Dependency*, April 6, 2015

with the demands of pregnancy or parenting."[8] The FY 2022 NDAA mandate is not only a policy change but also a cultural one. Thus, guidance is especially important for smoothing the transition, promoting equitable and unbiased practices, and preventing disparate impacts (e.g., conscious or unconscious bias steering racial and ethnic minority and/or women parents toward enlistment rather than retention in the officer pipeline, or paternalism toward white women who are pregnant but questioning the need for accommodations by pregnant women of color). The remainder of this section discusses the policy questions that could arise because of the NDAA requirement.

[8] CC-20-12, 2020, p. 2.

Dependents

DoDI 1322.22 states, "Those appointed as cadets or midshipmen must not have dependents,"[9] and it defines *dependency* as "[a]ny person for whom an individual has a legally recognized obligation to provide support including but not limited to spouse and natural, adoptive, or stepchildren."[10] In contrast, DoDI 1215.08, which governs the Senior ROTC, has no such dependency or marital rules for reserve cadets and midshipmen in ROTC programs across civilian colleges and universities.[11] ROTC cadets and midshipmen pursue an undergraduate degree in a participating college or university. Like other students, they need to meet academic degree requirements, but they also take ROTC-specific courses (e.g., Naval Science) and participate in ROTC training. ROTC does not prevent cadets or midshipmen from contracting or accepting scholarships because of marriage and dependency (up to a certain number of dependents). ROTC's guidance regarding dependents focuses on ensuring that the cadet or midshipman can balance duties, school, and parental responsibilities. Both DoDI 1322.22 and DoDI 1215.08 reference the medical standards for military service appointment from DoDI 6130.03 and state that their cadets and midshipmen must meet these standards.[12] Therefore, the guidelines surrounding pregnancy apply to both groups. However, the MSAs and ROTC differ in the guidelines for whether marriage or dependency disqualify someone for admission.

The FY 2022 NDAA requires that MSA cadets and midshipmen be allowed to become a biological parent while enrolled but is silent on other policy questions relating to dependents.

Policy Questions

- When revising DoDI 1322.22, should DoD consider lifting the prohibition on cadets and midshipmen being married?
  - If the prohibition is lifted, will anyone be able to marry, or only cadets and midshipmen who become biological parents while enrolled?
  - If the prohibition is not lifted, cadets and midshipmen who become parents while at the MSA will be required to remain single parents.
- Should DoD consider allowing cadets and midshipmen to enter the MSAs if they already have children?
  - If this allowance is not made, there would be an odd discontinuity at enrollment in that a cadet or midshipman would not be allowed to have a child the day before enrollment but would be allowed to have one the day after enrollment.

---

[9] DoDI 1322.22, 2015, p. 10.

[10] DoDI 1322.22, 2015, p. 21.

[11] DoDI 1215.08, *Senior Reserve Officers' Training Corps (ROTC) Programs*, U.S. Department of Defense, January 19, 2017, change 1, March 7, 2018.

[12] DoDI 1322.22, 2015; DoDI 1215.08, 2018; DoDI 6130.03, Vol. 1, *Medical Standards for Military Service: Appointment, Enlistment, or Induction*, U.S. Department of Defense, May 6, 2018, change 4, November 16, 2022.

  - If this allowance is not made, will waivers be available to retain students who were without dependents when they were accepted into the MSA but who are pregnant on enrollment?
- If the marriage prohibition for cadets and midshipmen is lifted or dependents are allowed on entry, will DoD align dependent policies for MSAs with active-duty policies so that adoptive children and stepchildren are eligible for the same protections and supports as biological children?

None of the service representatives we met with knew of any data that might indicate whether the dependent prohibition has deterred well-qualified civilians or enlisted personnel from applying to the MSAs. But removing this restriction could open up a wider pool of talent to the MSAs.

Pay and Benefits

Cadets and midshipmen are categorized as active-duty personnel in some respects but not in others. For example, they are counted as part of the active-component end strength,[13] and they are subject to the Uniform Code of Military Justice,[14] but they do not earn leave,[15] and their time as cadets and midshipmen does not count toward their length of military service.[16] Furthermore, unlike other active-duty personnel, cadets and midshipmen have been prohibited from having dependents. Therefore, laws on military dependent–related pays and benefits—such as health care, basic allowance for housing, and family separation allowance—have not specifically mentioned whether MSA cadet and midshipman dependents are included.[17] Now that new regulations will allow these students to have biological children as dependents, will there be legal and DoD policy changes that mirror or match pay and benefits available to active-duty dependents, or will cadets and midshipmen be called out as exceptions?

---

[13] DoDI, 1120.11 *Programming and Accounting for Active Component (AC) Military Manpower*, U.S. Department of Defense, March 17, 2015, p. 5.

[14] U.S. Code, Title 10, Armed Forces; Subtitle A, General Military Law; Part II, Personnel; Chapter 47, Uniform Code of Military Justice; Subchapter I, General Provisions; Section 802, Article 2: Persons Subject to This Chapter.

[15] U.S. Code, Title 10, Section 702(c) states that Sections 701, 703, and 704 regarding personnel leave do not apply to academy cadets or midshipmen.

[16] U.S. Code, Title 10, Armed Forces; Subtitle A, General Military Law; Part II, Personnel; Chapter 49, Miscellaneous Prohibitions and Penalties; Section 971, Service Credit: Officers May Not Count Service Performed While Serving as Cadet or Midshipman.

[17] For example, U.S. Code, Title 37, Pay and Allowances of the Uniformed Services; Chapter 3, Basic Pay; Section 203, Rates; and U.S. Code, Title 10, Armed Forces; Subtitle A, General Military Law; Part II, Personnel; Chapter 55, Medical and Dental Care.

Policy Questions

- Will cadets and midshipmen be eligible for any paid or unpaid parental leave?
- Will cadets and midshipmen with children be eligible for additional pay?[18]
- Will these children be eligible for Defense Enrollment Eligibility Reporting System (DEERS) enrollment and TRICARE health care coverage?
- Will these children's caregivers be given a military ID and access to the MSA installation to facilitate parent-child interaction during the cadets' and midshipmen's limited free time?
- If cadets and midshipmen are allowed to marry the co-parent, will that spouse be eligible for DEERS enrollment and TRICARE health care coverage?

Each of these considerations about whether to seek parity with other active-duty populations will have cost implications, which we discuss in Chapter 4.

Family Care

Parenthood could greatly add to the individual responsibilities of cadets and midshipmen. DoDI 1342.19 requires active-duty personnel with dependents to "plan for contingencies in the care and support of dependent family members" and "develop and submit a family care plan."[19] Such plans help prepare for caregiving arrangements when service members need to deploy, participate in extended field exercises, or travel for temporary duties or in cases of their serious injury, illness, or death. That same DoDI requires commanders to ensure that family care plans are up to date.[20] Cadets and midshipmen who become parents will need to make arrangements for care of their infant or toddler while they are attending school and could benefit from a well-considered contingency plan. This family care plan DoDI was last updated in 2017, however, and would need to be updated to describe how such a requirement would apply to cadets and midshipmen and their leaders.[21]

Also important for family care: Will DoD make the dependent-related supports of the Military Family Readiness System available to cadets and midshipmen and their dependents?[22] DoDI 1342.22 explains, "The mission of the [Military Family Readiness System] is to help

[18] The law states that cadets and midshipmen are entitled to pay "at the monthly rate equal to 35 percent of the basic pay of a commissioned officer in the pay grade O-1 with less than two years of service" and does not mention the possibility of an increase for cadets and midshipmen who become parents (U.S. Code, Title 37, Section 203).

[19] DoDI 1342.19, *Family Care Plans*, U.S. Department of Defense, May 7, 2010, change 1, November 30, 2017, p. 2.

[20] DoDI 1342.19, 2017, p. 2.

[21] DoDI 1342.19, 2017.

[22] For more information on these supports, see DoDI 1342.22, *Military Family Readiness*, U.S. Department of Defense, August 5, 2021; and Kenneth W. Kizer and Suzanne Le Menestrel, eds., *Strengthening the Military Family Readiness System for a Changing American Society*, National Academies Press, 2019.

Service members and family members with the challenges of daily living experienced in the unique context of military lifestyle,"[23] and it specifies that all service members are eligible for it.[24] The rationale for this system is that "[m]ilitary family well-being contributes to retention, resilience, readiness, and quality of life."[25] The programs and services that make up this system are quite diverse, supporting career, social, financial, health, and community domains. Some of these resources, as well as other possible supports, might be particularly valuable for cadets and midshipmen who are managing the stressors of becoming new parents, being physically separated from their children, supporting a child with a small stipend, and coordinating with co-parents and other caregivers—all on top of the demands of an MSA education.

Policy Questions

- Will cadets and midshipmen also be required to develop family care plans?
- Will cadets and midshipmen who become parents be eligible for other family support programs, such as new parent classes from the Family Advocacy Program?
- If the child of a cadet or midshipman has special medical or educational needs, will enrollment in the Exceptional Family Member Program be mandatory, as it is for other active-duty personnel?

Family care plans, new parent classes, and the Exceptional Family Member Program are about helping service members adjust to their roles, plan for the unexpected, and ensure that their child receives essential care. Offering these supports to cadet and midshipman parents may assist them in balancing their duties, school, and parental responsibilities.

Housing and Child Care

As noted in Chapter 1, cadets and midshipmen must live in dorms on the MSA campus. The rooms include basic furniture: primarily, twin beds; desks with chairs; shelves; a sink; and very limited storage for clothes, equipment, or personal belongings. The dorms are separate from faculty or staff government or privatized housing available on or near campus, including apartments, townhouses, and single-family homes.

The option for parents to live with or near their child, and possibly a co-parent, could help ensure that cadets and midshipmen are meeting their individual responsibilities to the child and the child's primary caregiver.

Furthermore, child care could be critical for ensuring that cadets and midshipmen meet their academic and professional responsibilities. DoD's Child Development Centers provide child care on military installations for active-duty personnel's infants and preschool-age chil-

[23] DoDI 1342.22, 2021, p. 11.

[24] DoDI 1342.22, 2021, pp. 5, 55.

[25] DoDI 1342.22, 2021, p. 14.

dren; certified family child care providers offer care in their homes on or near an installation; and a fee assistance program (a subsidy) helps families who do not live near DoD child care or are on a waitlist for it.[26]

The person with physical custody of the cadet or midshipman's child might have their own home and/or job away from the MSA; it should not be assumed they would all want to live on or near the MSA or near military facilities.

Policy Questions

- Will cadets and midshipmen who are parents be eligible for family housing on campus?
- Will they be allowed to live near campus with their child and potentially a co-parent?
- Will cadets and midshipmen whose children live close to the MSA be permitted to have cars (regardless of their year in school) and additional liberty passes?
- Will they be eligible to use the child development centers or family child care providers or receive a child care subsidy?
- Will co-parents be eligible for respite care?

Our meetings with MSA representatives highlighted the complexities surrounding any potential changes to housing policies or child care benefits for cadets or midshipmen with dependents. Although outside the scope of this study, future research could evaluate considerations regarding military family housing options on or near campus, including

- appropriateness of mixing cadet and midshipman families with the families of faculty and staff
- potential impact of additional demand on family housing or child care availability for faculty and staff
- feasibility and costs of building new family housing or converting existing buildings into cadet or midshipman family housing
- impact on privilege policies for cadets and midshipmen (e.g., liberty, having a car)
- potential impact on the education and military training because of housing cadets and midshipmen who are parents separately from their nonparent peers.

Managing Medical and Physical Aspects of Pregnancy, Childbirth, and Postpartum Experiences

Pregnant cadets and midshipmen may require some modifications to their activities or schedules. In anticipation of new DoD policies in response to the FY 2022 NDAA, the Department of the Air Force already has revised some of its policy. USAFA now allows cadets to stay at USAFA while pregnant, as DAFI 36-3501 states, "There is no prohibition on a cadet remain-

[26] For more details on DoD's child care programs, see Military OneSource "Military Child Care Programs," webpage, undated.

ing at USAFA while pregnant or after giving birth to a child."[27] This guidance states that accommodations must be made but provides none of the details found in policies covering non-cadet active-duty personnel.

Guidance regarding managing pregnancy, childbirth, and postpartum needs and limitations along with MSA academic and training requirements could promote consistent and equitable treatment. Without guidance, individuals' conscious or unconscious biases and lack of expert knowledge could lead to counterproductive and even discriminatory behavior by instructors, such as paternalism (e.g., unnecessarily restricting activities), pushing physical limits of pregnant cadets and midshipmen or having them work in unsafe conditions, or being dismissive of reported pain.

Cadets and midshipmen who are becoming fathers may also have interests or needs relating to attendance of the birth of the child; care for their co-parent before, during, and after childbirth; or care for an infant born with special medical needs or requiring extended hospitalization.

Policy Questions

- At what point in the pregnancy should the cadet or midshipman be *allowed* to take leave? At what point should they be *required* to take leave?
- Will there be broad or MSA-specific policy adjustments to physical fitness and training requirements for pregnant cadets and midshipmen? For example, will there be changes to fitness standards, testing, group physical training (e.g., combat survival training, sea trials, obstacle courses, tear gas training, swimming and water survival tests)?
  - Will pregnant cadets be prevented from participating in certain activities? Given the choice to opt out? Be required to make up later anything that was missed?
- Will pregnant students be excused from class for medical appointments and be able to get transportation if they need to receive care in town, which could be a long distance from their dorm?
- Will students who are fathering a child be excused to attend pregnancy-related medical appointments with their co-parent? Will they be excused to attend the birth of their child?
- Will there be physical or schedule accommodations for pregnancy and postpartum needs (related to, for example, bedrest, morning sickness, or lactation)?

The policies and procedures in place for active-duty personnel could serve as an example of what could be implemented at the MSAs. For example, Army Directive 2022-06 has an entire section on physical fitness following pregnancy that could be referenced.[28] In addition to details on physical fitness, the directive offers detailed guidance on lactation accommoda-

[27] DAFI 36-3501, 2022, p.42.

[28] Army Directive 2022-06, *Parenthood, Pregnancy, and Postpartum*, Department of the Army, April 19, 2022, pp. 1–2.

tions and postpartum body composition exemptions. Soldiers are exempt from the physical fitness test while pregnant and 12 months after the end of pregnancy, and they are exempt from other physical readiness requirements (e.g., unit physical training) for 180 days after the end of pregnancy. Notably, soldiers may participate in physical fitness and readiness activities during the period they are exempt, and they are encouraged to do so within their limits.

However, certain policies and case-by-case decisions may need to be made locally and must take into account the particular circumstances of the individual cadet or midshipman, the MSA, and the surrounding community. For example, USMA leadership explained to us that West Point's Keller Army Community Hospital no longer has obstetrics and gynecology capabilities or labor and delivery services for its 750 Army families, let alone for any cadets who become pregnant. Outsourcing to regional medical centers has put such health care approximately 45 minutes away from USMA, making the logistical issues nontrivial.

Leaves of Absence

U.S. Code, Title 10 authorizes DoD to make MSA leave policies: "The Secretary concerned, or his designated representative, may prescribe regulations relating to leave for cadets and midshipmen."[29] The policies already include details on administrative and medical leave, and cadets and midshipmen are already permitted to take leave to manage a pregnancy as long as they return without having a dependent. However, the FY 2022 NDAA requirement raises questions about whether these policies should be modified—both during the period of pregnancy and afterward—or whether more-detailed guidance is required.

Moreover, DoD has granted all active-duty members a minimum of 12 weeks of paid parental leave relating to a qualifying birth event.[30] The Department of the Air Force has already updated its policies to make this expanded leave available to Air Force and Space Force personnel.[31] The period of leave does not have to be taken all at once, allowing service members to take partial parental leave at different increments.

Policy Questions

- Will cadets and midshipmen be required to take a leave of absence while pregnant?
- Will health care be covered during the absence for biological mothers?[32] What about for biological fathers?
- Does DoD's parental leave policy apply to cadets and midshipmen?

[29] U.S. Code, Title 10, Section 702.

[30] Department of Defense Directive-Type Memorandum 23-001, *Expansion of the Military Parental Leave Program*, U.S. Department of Defense, January 4, 2023.

[31] This expanded leave initially appeared in Department of the Air Force Guidance Memorandum 2022-01 to DAFI 36-3003, *Military Leave Program*, Department of the Air Force, January 5, 2023a, and remained in the subsequent update (March 30, 2023b).

[32] For the purposes of this report, we use the term *mother* to refer to the cadet or midshipman who becomes pregnant.

- Will cadets and midshipmen receive a stipend during the absence?
- What is the maximum length of absence?
- Can emergency absences be granted to deal with child emergencies?
- If cadets and midshipmen receive an extra year of stipend and/or TRICARE for the birth of a child, will there be an additional service obligation?
- Could cadets and midshipmen serve as enlisted active-duty members during a leave of absence and thus be eligible for full benefits while working and continuing their preparation for a military career?

These policy questions are not unprecedented. At the USMA, under AR 150-1, cadets who acquire a physical disability or medical condition can be granted up to one year of medical leave, and the Commandant of Cadets decides whether they will continue to be paid.[33] The USMA representatives we met with reported that medical leave has already been used with pregnant cadets.

Prompting the last policy question listed here, the MSAs have programs that could be modified to include cadets and midshipmen who become parents: the Midshipmen Reevaluation and Reappointment Program at USNA,[34] the Mentorship Reevaluation Readmission Program at USAFA,[35] and the Mentorship Program at USMA.[36] These programs give MSA leadership options for addressing cadets or midshipmen who stumbled in their performance amid an otherwise strong record. The cadets and midshipmen are placed on enlisted status but with the potential to reapply to return after a set period or completing an enlisted term of service. These programs could be a model for transitioning new parents to enlisted status while leaving the door open for a potential return.

Disenrollment, Resignation, and Recoupment

DoDI 1322.22 states, "Active-duty service is the primary means of reimbursement for education. Cadets and midshipmen disenrolling or those disenrolled after the beginning of the third academic year from a Service academy normally will be called to active duty in enlisted status, if fit for service."[37] However, not everyone is fit for service. This same DoDI explains, "Individuals failing to complete the required course of academy instruction (including disenrollment for academics, conduct, honor code violations, or physical deficiency) will be disenrolled."[38] If disenrolled and unable to be ordered to active duty, cadets and midshipmen

[33] AR 150-1, 2021.

[34] SECNAVINST 1531.4A, 2018.

[35] Communication from a USAFA representative, December 2022.

[36] AR 150-1, 2021, p. 24.

[37] DoDI 1322.22, 2015, p.2.

[38] DoDI 1322.22, 2015, p. 14.

may be required to reimburse the U.S. government for the cost of their education, a process known as *recoupment*.[39] This reimbursement requirement is not applicable prior to the commencement of the third year of education. Similar guidelines exist for ROTC disenrollments.[40]

Under the dependent prohibition, MSA cadets and midshipmen wanting to retain their parental rights (and thus would have to leave the MSA) could request transfer to an ROTC program in lieu of reimbursement or enlisted service, as stated in DoDI 1322.22:

> U.S. cadets or midshipman who resign or are disenrolled for violation of the dependency policy may request transfer to the Reserve Officer Training Corps (ROTC). Approval and method of transfer is at the discretion of the Secretary of the Military Department concerned. Cadets and midshipmen who are approved to transfer to ROTC, graduate, receive a commission, and fulfill their Active Duty Service Obligation (ADSO) are not subject to reimbursement as outlined in this section.[41]

This option is allowed at the discretion of the MSA leadership and/or higher leadership at the military department.

Policy Questions

- With DoD's new policy, under what circumstances (if any) would cadets and midshipmen be involuntarily disenrolled because of disruptions caused by parenting responsibilities?
- Should there be any uniform guidelines for recoupment or service obligation for cadets or midshipmen who become parents (e.g., recoupment waived for all parents)?
- Will health care costs, additional stipends, or other benefits be factored into recoupment calculations?

We note that recoupment could present a significant hardship for cadet and midshipman parents leaving the MSA, who may be without a house, job, or college degree. If current practices reported to us by MSA representatives were to continue, waiver of recoupment and service decisions would be made on a case-by-case basis and would likely consider the cadet's or midshipman's record of performance and conduct.

Service Obligations and Officer Commissioning

Cadets and midshipmen receive free education and military professional development; in return, they incur an obligation to accept a commission as a military officer.

Officer commissioning standards already address pregnancy. The medical standards for entrance into the military per DoDI 6130.03 state that a disqualifying condition for entering

[39] DoDI 1322.22, 2015, p. 15.

[40] DoDI 1215.08, 2018, pp. 17-19.

[41] DoDI 1322.22, 2015, p. 16.

the military is "[p]regnancy through 6 months after the completion of the pregnancy,"[42] and DoDI 6130.03 emphasizes, "The DoD Components will consider disqualification for pregnancy as temporary."[43]

DoDI 1322.22 explains how cadets or midshipmen may be placed on a limited duty status if they are not medically qualified at their time of commissioning (for up to one year).[44] If, after this time has passed, they become medically qualified, they can be commissioned. If not, they may be subject to recoupment. DoDI 1322.22 also states,

> Cadets and midshipmen who become medically disqualified for appointment (including pregnancy) as a commissioned officer during their senior year, who otherwise would be qualified to complete the course of instruction and be appointed as a commissioned officer, and who are capable of completing the academic course of instruction with their peers, may be permitted by the Secretary of the Military Department concerned to complete the academic course of instruction with award of an academic credential.[45]

Thus, the policies allow for a defined gap between graduation from the academy and commissioning as an officer for pregnant cadets and midshipmen. This raises questions about whether a break between leaving an MSA without graduating and beginning a service obligation would be feasible and permissible.

Policy Questions

- Can parents who leave the MSA without graduating request a break before service must begin? For example, if a student were leaving the MSA without graduating and preparing to transition to enlisted status, could they request a defined break of up to one year before they had to begin their term of service (to allow for childbirth and time to care for an infant)?
  - If a break is permitted, what health care coverage or other supports would they have, if any, during that gap?
- If the government provides for health care and/or a stipend during such a break, will the service obligation increase?
- Will the government facilitate an application and transfer to an ROTC unit with a scholarship, or is this entirely the responsibility of the cadet or midshipman parent?

To the last point, our research sponsor noted to us that, to date, the cadets and midshipmen who became parents have been responsible for finding a school and ROTC unit that would accept them—a challenge even without a new baby to prepare and care for. However, there is

42 DoDI 6130.03, Vol. 1, 2022, p. 28.

43 DoDI 6130.03, Vol. 1, 2022, p. 4.

44 DoDI 1322.22, 2015, p. 18.

45 DoDI 1322.22, 2015, p. 16.

precedent for military department assistance with transfers. As required by Section 555 of the FY 2020 NDAA, DoD and the military departments developed procedures for assisting sexual assault victims with expedited transfers from MSAs to ROTC detachments at other colleges and universities.[46] Thus, DoD could consider offering similar support to new parents to help retain them in the officer pipeline.

Transfer to ROTC would not address the challenges of obtaining income or health care to support the parent and child, however the greater flexibility could be invaluable and even essential for some parents. For example, ROTC cadets and midshipmen can live with their children, live with or near a co-parent or another caregiver, transport themselves and their children to medical appointments, and have more control over their daily schedules.

Key Findings and Conclusions

In this chapter, we discuss many possible policy decisions that could stem from the required change in the FY 2022 NDAA.

DoD's policy options vary: (1) making minimal changes to comply with the FY 2022 NDAA; (2) creating standardized guidance to address implementation issues; (3) providing additional pays, benefits, programs, and services to support the parent and child; and (4) lifting other prohibitions, such as those on cadet and midshipman marriage, having children on entering, and having other types of dependents. At the time of this writing, DoD's approach to creating guidance is to ensure consistent implementation, and the relevant DoDI 1322.22 is expected to be updated in 2023. DoD could consider offering benefits and services that align with those provided to other active-duty personnel (e.g., health care, child care, family housing, and new parent support programs). Here, we highlight our key findings across the military policy landscape.

Changing DoD Policy to Allow Cadets and Midshipmen to Preserve Their Parental Rights Presents Multiple Opportunities to Protect the Pipeline for Incoming Officer Talent

The Section 559A requirement provides an opportunity for DoD to consider additional policy questions relating to parental rights to ensure the pipeline for officer talent remains strong.[47] The policy options discussed in this chapter may present a significant culture shift in some domains compared with the current practice at the academies. Some of the options, particularly those surrounding pays and benefits, have cost implications, which we delve into

---

[46] Information on the FY 2020 NDAA is drawn from U.S. Department of Defense, *Annual Report on Sexual Harassment and Violence at the Military Service Academies: Academic Program Year 2020–2021*, February 15, 2022, p. 32.

[47] Public Law 117-81, Section 559A, 2021.

further in the next chapter. Despite the potential costs and challenges in implementing this change, the new policy also presents an opportunity for DoD to preserve—or perhaps even expand—the pool of talented officers commissioning from the MSAs. If additional supports or changes in practices provide a better foundation for cadet and midshipman parents to succeed, these shifts could lead to higher retention and additional high-quality military officers. The changes in policy could also be designed in a way that links additional privileges for parents to service obligations or enables parents to transition to ROTC or enlisted service more flexibly to accommodate their responsibilities as parents with their military careers.

The Many Possible Ways Section 559A Could Be Implemented Indicate the Need for a Strategic Plan to Roll Out the New Policies

Some of the policy questions raised in this chapter focus on local practices that could vary across the MSAs (e.g., excused absences, additional liberty). Because there are so many possible ways for the FY 2022 NDAA requirement to be implemented, it will be important for DoD and the MSAs to have a plan for rolling out policy changes and to ensure that faculty, staff, instructors, commanders, cadets, and midshipmen are aware of these changes. Clear and consistent dissemination of information surrounding the new policy will also help with the culture shift.

Certain MSA Policies Are Already Aligned with or Applicable to Section 559A Changes

The update to DoDI 1322.22 is expected to be released in 2023, and corresponding changes to military department and MSA policies and practices are expected to follow. We note here that certain MSA policies are already aligned with or applicable to the new requirements. For example, in anticipation of the forthcoming DoDI revision, DAFI 36-3501 was updated in 2022 to say that pregnant cadets can stay at the USAFA.[48] This guidance states generally that accommodations must be made, but details are not yet provided. At the USMA, under the authority of AR 150-1, pregnant cadets have previously been granted up to one year of medical leave, and the Commandant of Cadets decides whether the cadets will continue to receive their stipend during this period.[49] The USNA Midshipmen Reevaluation and Reappointment Program could be a model for putting parents on enlisted status, then allowing them to reapply to return after/within one year.[50] USAFA reported that its Mentorship Reevaluation Readmission Program is a similar two-year program of enlisted service. USMA also has

---

[48] DAFI 36-3501, 2022.

[49] AR 150-1, 2021, p. 43. USNA and USAFA representatives report the use of unpaid administrative leave for pregnant cadets but a lack of policy providing a medical leave option with authority to approve a continued stipend.

[50] SECNAVINST 1531.4A, 2018.

a mentorship program through which the superintendent can invite former cadets to apply for readmission after enlisted active duty service.[51] Planned or anticipated length of enlisted service and medical status of the cadet or midshipman will likely shape what occupational specialties are practical; occupational training timelines and physical requirements vary.

Tracking, Monitoring, and Evaluating the Implementation and Effect of New Policies Will Enable Early Corrections and Refinements

Implementation of new policy could be challenging, and the challenges could evolve over time. By planning to track, monitor, and evaluate the effects of policy changes, DoD and the military departments will be well positioned to make data-informed adjustments to policy and practice. If needed, adjustments and refinements could target better outcomes in areas such as retention, academic performance, and well-being of the child and parent; these adjustments also could prevent bias in how cadet and midshipman parents are treated and rated. Senior leader guidance on how to manage these issues could help prevent inconsistency and dangerous or discriminatory actions.

[51] AR 150-1, 2021, p. 24.

CHAPTER 4

Cost Implications

The final task in this project was to estimate potential costs of administering various policy options for cadets and midshipmen who retain their parental rights. Potential costs could include increased use of existing benefits and additional pay or benefits to help support the health and welfare of the dependent child or family as a unit. To provide insight on potential costs, we model the cost under six scenarios with varying levels of benefits and pay provided to the cadet or midshipman parent and their families. In this chapter, we describe our approach and provide results on the potential magnitude of these costs.

Estimation Approach

Broadly, there are two main inputs for deriving cost estimates: an estimate of the number of cadets and midshipmen who might become parents while they are students and an estimate of the costs of supports needed by cadets and midshipmen who are parents. We initially planned to estimate costs using the number of cadet and midshipman parents observed in historical data as a reference. However, we learned from MSA representatives that no reliable, centralized data source exists that captures how many cadets and midshipmen become parents each year, and there has been no requirement to collect, analyze, or report on such data. Also, identifying new instances of parenthood is challenging in cases in which the new pregnancy is not obvious or in which the father is a cadet or midshipman and the mother is not. Moreover, cadets and midshipmen have faced a disincentive when it comes to reporting pregnancy or parenthood status: Having dependents has been a policy violation that can lead to disenrollment, and no dependent benefits have been available. As a result, a count of known cases would be merely anecdotal and likely a serious undercount.

Therefore, we adjusted our approach and instead estimated the costs for one cadet or midshipman under different scenarios, for which we included varying levels of supports. We present analyses estimating costs for cadets and midshipmen who become parents in each year while they are at the academy. The health care costs for cadets and midshipmen who give birth will differ from the health care costs of cadets and midshipmen who biologically father a child with a civilian.[1] Adding to that differential, for cost estimation purposes, we also calculated the TRICARE health care costs for a potential year of absence for pregnant cadets and midshipmen but not for cadets and midshipmen who father a child. In reality, there may be cases of fathers taking leave, and, overall, some of the cadets and midshipmen who become parents might take a leave of absence for only one semester. The approach to estimating costs for the subsequent years after the leave of absence are the same for all cadet and midshipman parents. To consider the implications if admissions policies regarding dependents were to be changed, we model an option in which cadets and midshipmen can enter the academy with a child. When there was a range for the potential value of a particular cost (e.g., health care costs), we chose the highest value in the range to estimate an upper bound. We also model costs for an entire year during the year of birth, when, in reality, only a partial year of costs may be needed, depending on when during the year the child is born. This decision also would lead to an upper bound in our estimates.

The estimates on a per-person basis may be aggregated to examine how the costs may change if different numbers of cadets or midshipmen were to become parents. We present aggregated estimates in a scenario in which ten cadets or midshipmen in a given cohort become parents during their tenure at the academy. The true number of cadet or midshipman parents in each year is unknown, and it is unknown how these numbers may shift after the change in policy. The aggregated estimates are intended only to provide a benchmark for understanding the overall magnitude of potential costs. Readers can infer from the per-person estimates how the costs would change if the number of cadet or midshipman parents is larger or smaller than the aggregate estimate provided in this report.

Finally, to provide context for the magnitude of our estimates, we provide several cost benchmarks for comparison, including the total cost of education for one graduating cadet or midshipman, the total cost of education for a cohort of graduating cadets and midshipmen, and total health care costs for one graduating cadet or midshipman and a cohort of graduating cadets and midshipmen. We also discuss the implications for changes in recoupment.

Supports Included in the Scenarios

As discussed in Chapter 3, there are a variety of DoD policy options with cost implications. We only model scenarios in which new parents have one child, which we expect to be typical, although multiples (e.g., twins, multiple pregnancies) are possible and would increase costs.[2]

The first scenario that we model represents the increased use of an existing benefit only: health care for cadets and midshipmen. Pregnant cadets and midshipmen have already had the option to take a one-year leave of absence from the MSAs: The policy question is whether

[1] If the partner who gives birth is on active duty, such as a cadet or midshipman who graduated ahead of the father, then that cost is already covered by pay and benefits provided to service members with dependents.

[2] Readers interested in estimating the costs for multiple children may be able to infer these costs from the annual cost of specific supports listed in Table 4.2.

their TRICARE costs would be covered during this absence. For this scenario, our estimates focus on the TRICARE costs associated with a one-year leave of absence, including covering the pregnancy, childbirth, and postpartum period. The second scenario examines how the costs would change if cadets and midshipmen were allowed to continue to collect a monthly stipend during a yearlong leave of absence.

Alternative scenarios build on these base costs, adding increasing levels of pay and benefits. We prioritized including the costs for supplemental income, health care, and child care subsidies. These represent increased costs for the parent or for supporting the child, since the FY 2022 NDAA focused on "a cadet or midshipman who becomes pregnant or fathers a child while attending a military service academy."[3] Moreover, if authorized and funded, these policy options are also relatively easy to implement; systems are already in place to issue stipends to cadets and midshipmen, provide health care to service members and dependents, and provide child care subsidies to active-duty personnel.

The additional pay and benefits included in alternative scenarios will include newborn costs and dependent TRICARE coverage for the child because extending health care benefits would enable cadets and midshipmen to meet the child's basic health needs. We also model the cost of an additional stipend provided to cadet and midshipman parents with the intent to assist with financial support for the child. We set the cost of the additional stipend to be equal to the current stipend provided to cadets and midshipmen, an option that has been proposed within DoD. We include the cost of this stipend during the year of absence for cadets and midshipmen who give birth, as well as in all subsequent years when they return to the MSA after becoming a parent.

Another factor for our scenarios is the cost of child care assistance when the cadets and midshipmen are not on a leave of absence. We estimate the cost of child care assistance to be equal to the maximum child care subsidy provided to active-duty members who are unable to access on-base providers.[4] We do not include child care costs during the year of absence for cadets and midshipmen who give birth but do include nine months of child care costs in the first year of the child's life for cadets and midshipmen who father a child with a civilian.

The health care and child care costs included in the six scenarios that we modeled are summarized as follows (see Table 4.1):

- Scenario 1 covers only the additional TRICARE health care costs for the pregnant/childbearing cadet or midshipmen during a one-year leave of absence from the MSA, including pregnancy, childbirth, and postpartum costs.

---

3 Public Law 117-81, Section 559A, 2021.

4 In reality, the actual child care subsidy depends on many factors, including the location, cost of the civilian child care option, and age and number of children. The decision to model child care assistance with the maximum subsidy likely leads to an upper-bound estimate because not all cadets or midshipmen would receive the maximum stipend, and some may not require a child care subsidy at all.

TABLE 4.1
Summary of Six Modeling Scenarios

Costs for . . .	Included Cost	Scenarios 1	2	3	4	5	6
Cadet/midshipman	TRICARE coverage for cadet/midshipman during pregnancy, childbirth, postpartum, and one-year leave of absence	X	X	X	X	X	X
	Regular stipend during one year of absence		X		X	X	X
Child	TRICARE coverage for newborn in hospital and for child dependent			X	X	X	X
	Additional stipend to assist with child expenses					X	X
	Child care subsidy						X

- Scenario 2 adds on the cost of continuing the cadet and midshipman regular stipend during the leave of absence.
- Scenario 3 focuses on TRICARE health care coverage only, including the costs in Scenario 1 as well as health care coverage for the newborn while in the hospital and regular dependent coverage after the child leaves the hospital.
- Scenario 4 combines Scenarios 2 and 3, including all TRICARE health care costs for the cadet or midshipman who gives birth and for their child, as well as the regular stipend during a leave of absence.
- Scenarios 5 and 6 add the cost of additional supports for the child, first adding a stipend to help cover child expenses (5), then adding a child care subsidy (6).

The FY 2022 NDAA does not mention lifting the marriage prohibition for cadets and midshipmen, but, for reference, we consider an option that would more closely align with policies for other active-duty personnel who are allowed to have spouses and children eligible for health care and child care benefits. We will provide alternative results for Scenarios 3 through 6, which also include the costs of extending TRICARE coverage to a dependent civilian spouse. When a cadet or midshipman fathers a child, these health care costs for the dependent spouse include the costs of pregnancy and childbirth for spouses who give birth.

Additional Supports Not Included in the Models

Our analyses are based on scenarios in which cadets and midshipman continue to live in dorms on campus and do not have physical custody of their children. As discussed in Chapter 3, evaluating the policy and cost implications of changes to housing options at the MSAs would require a more substantial effort than was feasible within this project.

We prioritized the costs of the policy options that are likely to be most essential for parents: pay, health care, and child care. But active-duty military personnel who are parents also have access to a variety of other valuable supports that have cost implications. Although such supports are not included in our cost estimates, we acknowledge the potential costs associated with other supports that could be offered to cadets and midshipmen, such as adoption benefits, the Exceptional Family Member Program, or new parent support programs. We also did not model uniform costs (if pregnant cadets and midshipmen require maternity uniforms) or additional meal expenses (if pregnant or breastfeeding cadets and midshipmen require dietary changes that would result in higher costs).

Potential Savings or Cost Reductions Not Modeled

Several potential savings are not factored into our analyses. Cadet and midshipman parents may be eligible for tax credits and exemptions, including the Child Tax Credit, the Earned Income Tax Credit, Dependent Care Tax Credits, and increased dependent exemptions. These credits and exemptions may reduce the parents' costs of providing for the child and, to the extent that they reduce the member's taxable income, may reduce DoD's contributions to Social Security and Medicare, offering a savings to DoD. Given that cadet and midshipman income is relatively low, however, the savings to DoD are likely to be relatively small.

Additionally, there could be cases in which the costs would be lower than our estimates. For example, if both parents were cadets or midshipmen, TRICARE for the child would not be double counted, and, depending on policy decisions, other supports (such as a supplemental stipend to assist with child care costs) might not be doubled. Pregnancies could also end in miscarriages, stillbirths, and newborn deaths, which would reduce the cost estimates for supports for the children.

Data Sources

We relied on several public data sources, as well as aggregated data provided by the MSAs to estimate the cost inputs (Table 4.2). We obtained information about TRICARE costs for dependents, maternity care, and newborn care from the Defense Health Agency (DHA)'s TRICARE 2021 annual evaluation.[5] To derive the cost of the additional child stipend, we obtained information about cadet and midshipman basic pay and stipend amounts from FY 2022 MSA budget books and DFAS.[6] For the alternative scenarios, we used the 2022 child

[5] DHA, *Evaluation of the TRICARE Program: Fiscal Year 2021 Report to Congress: Access, Cost, and Quality Data Through Fiscal Year 2020*, U.S. Department of Defense, February 26, 2021; DHA, *Evaluation of the TRICARE Program: Fiscal Year 2022 Report to Congress: Access, Cost, and Quality Data Through Fiscal Year 2021*, U.S. Department of Defense, February 28, 2022; Defense Finance and Accounting Service (DFAS), "Monthly Rates of Basic Pay—Effective January 1, 2022," U.S. Department of Defense, 2022.

[6] USNA, "Midshipman Stipend and Annual Budget Book: Academic Year 2022–2023," Department of the Navy, May 19, 2022; U.S. Military Academy, "2020 Cost of Education for Public Law 96-357," March 22, 2021.

TABLE 4.2
Inputs for Cost Estimates

Cost Input	Estimated Cost, 2022
TRICARE cost for cadet or midshipman for one pregnancy, childbirth, and postpartum period[a]	$6,203
TRICARE cost for cadet or midshipman during a one-year leave of absence[b]	$4,723
TRICARE cost for one newborn at the time of birth[a]	$6,437
TRICARE cost for one year of coverage for a dependent child or dependent civilian spouse[b]	$4,472
Additional stipend to help cover costs of supporting a child (twelve months)[c]	$14,604
Child care subsidy (twelve months)[d]	$20,400

[a] DHA, 2021.
[b] DHA, 2022.
[c] DFAS, 2022; USNA, 2022; Department of the Army, U.S. Military Academy, "Cadet Budget, Academic Year 2021–2022," August 2021.
[d] Child Care Aware of America, undated.

NOTE: TRICARE costs are derived from the DHA 2021 and 2022 TRICARE reports, which reflect costs from FY 2020 and FY 2021, using a 3.9-percent medical inflation rate and 2.6-percent inflation rate for other items to convert costs to 2022 dollars. TRICARE costs for pregnancy, childbirth, and postpartum and a newborn reflect the costs associated with one pregnancy and a newborn. All other costs listed above are annual costs.

care subsidy maximum per month for full-time care.[7] For additional context on potential costs and savings, we requested data from each MSA on the average amount of education costs recouped from cadets and midshipmen who disenrolled because of parental rights related reasons and, for students more broadly, the number who repaid any MSA education costs and the number for whom all MSA costs were waived.

Finally, we requested estimates of the total annual cost of education for a cadet or midshipman from the DoD Comptroller and each of the MSAs, which was reported as $90,981. These education costs include costs for faculty and staff, learning materials, housing, meals, medical expenses, and a stipend and FICA payroll tax for the cadets and midshipmen.

To derive the estimates of TRICARE costs for pregnancy, childbirth, postpartum care, and neonatal and/or newborn care, we took the aggregated total costs reported for these diagnosis groups and divided by the number of dispositions reported in the 2021 DHA report.[8] We used the reported costs for active-duty members for the costs of care for the cadet or midshipman during the leave of absence and used the reported costs for active-duty family members for the cost of dependents. However, the reported values did not distinguish between

[7] Child Care Aware of America, "DoD Fee Assistance," webpage, undated.

[8] Note that the 2022 report did not provide the detailed data on aggregate costs for pregnancy and a newborn to derive the per-student estimates as described here. We thus derive the individual pregnancy, childbirth, and postpartum and neonatal costs from the 2021 report, which lists costs and dispositions for FY 2020. Estimates of dependent costs and active-duty member costs are taken from the 2022 report (which provides FY 2021 costs). We then apply the medical inflation rate to inflate all costs to 2022 dollars.

the costs of active-duty family member adults and children. To obtain an annual estimate of TRICARE costs for both the cadet or midshipman and their dependents, we summed the average per person cost for inpatient, outpatient, and prescription care as reported in the 2021 report. For dependent care, we used the values in the report assuming a military treatment facility primary care manager (rather than assuming a network primary care manager or nonprime coverage, both of which yielded slightly lower total costs). The estimates for the other support items (stipend, child care, and academy education) were provided directly by the listed sources.

We report per-year values in 2022 dollars and present aggregates over multiple years in nominal dollars. When calculating costs for future years (e.g., in estimating the cost over all years of academy attendance for a cadet or midshipman who becomes a parent in their second year), we apply a 3.9-percent inflation rate to TRICARE costs and use an inflation rate of 2.6 percent to other expenses. These rates are based on rates that the DoD Comptroller's office uses in its budget projections.[9]

Results

The results of our cost assessment add up the per-parent, per-year costs listed in Table 4.2 for each of the scenarios shown in Table 4.1. We first aggregate costs across all years that a cadet or midshipman would be at the academy after becoming a parent, adjusting for inflation. For example, for a cadet or midshipman who becomes a parent in their first year, we aggregate costs across four (or five, in the case of a cadet or midshipman who takes a leave of absence) years; for someone who becomes a parent in their last year, we aggregate costs over only one (or two) years. We present totals separately for cadets or midshipmen who give birth and for cadets or midshipmen who father a child with a civilian. Next, we demonstrate how costs would change if TRICARE coverage were also extended to a civilian co-parent starting at the time of pregnancy. Because Scenarios 1 and 2 do not offer any TRICARE coverage for dependents, we calculate changes in cost for offering TRICARE to a civilian co-parent only for Scenarios 3 through 6. We also present totals for cadets and midshipmen who may enter the academy with a child (e.g., we exclude the costs associated with childbirth and the leave of absence). We then aggregate the numbers to a total of ten cadets and midshipmen.

Cost per Cadet or Midshipman

Table 4.3 shows the costs for additional supports under the various scenarios for a single cadet or midshipman in their first and last year at the academy, illustrating a range of the potential

[9] Office of the Under Secretary of Defense, Comptroller, *National Defense Budget Estimates for FY 2023*, U.S. Department of Defense, July 2022b.

TABLE 4.3

Cost for Additional Supports per Cadet or Midshipman Parent Under Various Scenarios

	Cadet/Midshipman Gives Birth		Cadet/Midshipman Co-Parent Gives Birth		Cadet/Midshipman Co-Parent Gives Birth, + Spouse TRICARE		Cadet/Midshipman Enters Academy with a Child
Year of Parenthood	Year 1	Year 4	Year 1	Year 4	Year 1	Year 4	Year 1
Scenario 1: TRICARE for birth costs + during leave of absence	$10,926	$10,926	—	—	—	—	—
Scenario 2: 1 + stipend during leave of absence	$25,530	$25,530	—	—	—	—	—
Scenario 3: 1 + TRICARE for child	$41,787	$26,733	$25,650	$11,160	$50,814	$21,835	$18,961
Scenario 4: 2 + 3	$56,391	$41,337	$25,650	$11,160	$50,814	$21,835	$18,961
Scenario 5: 4 + additional stipend	$133,308	$70,924	$86,384	$25,764	$111,548	$36,439	$79,695
Scenario 6: 5 + child care subsidy	$220,352	$91,855	$166,122	$41,064	$191,286	$51,739	$164,533

SOURCES: Costs were derived using data from DHA, 2021; DHA, 2022; DFAS, 2022; USNA, 2022; Department of the Army, U.S. Military Academy, 2021; Child Care Aware of America, undated; and estimates provided by DoD Comptroller's office.

NOTE: Costs in the year of birth are reported in 2022 dollars. Subsequent year costs are adjusted using a 3.9-percent medical inflation rate and 2.6-percent inflation rate for other expenses. Costs are estimated only for the additional support costs modeled in each scenario and do not include the standard costs of education for each cadet or midshipman.

costs (e.g., with four years and one year remaining in their education, respectively).[10] In each scenario, costs are higher for cadets and midshipmen who give birth—both because of the TRICARE costs associated with the pregnancy and childbirth and because of the cost of providing the regular stipend and additional supports for the child for an additional year during the leave of absence. Not surprisingly, costs are highest for a cadet or midshipman who gives birth during the first year and lowest for a cadet or midshipman who fathers a child in their last year at the academy.

Under all profiles, the costs for Scenarios 1 through 4—which focus only on TRICARE costs and the cadet's or midshipman's regular stipend during a one-year leave of absence—are under $60,000. The costs increase significantly once the additional stipend and child care subsidy are added. For reference, the cost of an additional stipend for five years (e.g., four years at the academy plus a one-year leave of absence) is approximately $77,000 after our

[10] The calculated costs for cadets and midshipmen having a child in each possible year at the academy are shown in Tables B.1 and B.2 in Appendix B.

adjustment for inflation. The cost of four years of child care is approximately $87,000 after adjusting for inflation. These costs exceed the costs of providing TRICARE for the cadet or midshipman or a dependent. But they also reflect the reality of financial demands that cadets and midshipmen will face as parents in raising their children.

The costs increase further when we include the costs of TRICARE for a civilian co-parent. In Table 4.3, we show the costs of TRICARE for a civilian co-parent who gives birth, but the reverse profile is shown in Appendix B. Adding the costs of pregnancy, childbirth, and postpartum plus one year of dependent coverage adds approximately $11,000 to the cost for a cadet or midshipman who fathers a child in their final year at the academy; adding the costs of pregnancy, childbirth, and postpartum plus four years of dependent coverage adds approximately $25,000 to the cost for a cadet or midshipman who fathers a child in their first year at the academy.

The costs for a cadet or midshipman who enters the academy with a child vary depending on the supports included. Because there is no cost of childbirth or leave of absence, the costs are zero under Scenarios 1 and 2. In Scenarios 3 and 4, costs only include health care coverage for the child (e.g., no stipend costs during a leave of absence) and are approximately $19,000 for four years at the academy. However, costs are significantly higher under Scenarios 5 and 6, at approximately $80,000 and $165,000, respectively. Costs increase significantly in these last two scenarios because the child stipend and child care subsidy would need to be provided for all four years that this cadet or midshipman attends the academy.

Therefore, although the costs for cadets and midshipmen who enter the academy with a child under Scenarios 3 and 4 are similar to those who have a child in their *last* year at the academy, the costs for cadets and midshipmen who enter the academy with a child under Scenarios 5 and 6 are similar to those who have a child in their *first* year at the academy. Because this profile abstracts from the costs associated with the birth of a child, it provides a clear example of the difference between the costs of providing health care and other financial supports.

Because of these varying factors, potential costs under various scenarios and profiles range widely from zero (e.g., Scenario 1 or 2 for a cadet or midshipman who fathers a child or who enters the academy with a child) or approximately $11,000 (when only the costs of a birth are covered) to approximately $220,000 (Scenario 6 for a first-year cadet or midshipman who gives birth).

Aggregate Costs of Various Scenarios

Table 4.4 aggregates the individual costs from Table 4.3, showing totals for ten cadet or midshipman parents. Demographic data from recent cohorts at each of the MSAs indicate that between 20 and 30 percent of recent entering classes were women. Therefore, for the purposes of aggregating the per-parent numbers, we include costs for three cadets and midshipmen who give birth and seven who father a child. For the profile in which the cadet or midshipman enters the academy with a child, there is no difference in cost across the ten individual

TABLE 4.4

Aggregated Costs for Additional Supports for Ten Cadet or Midshipman Parents Under Various Scenarios

	Ten Cadets/Midshipmen		Ten Cadets/Midshipmen + Spouse TRICARE		Ten Cadets/ Midshipmen Enter with a Child
Scenario	Year 1	Year 4	Year 1	Year 4	Year 1
Scenario 1: TRICARE for birth costs + during leave of absence	$32,778	$32,778	—	—	—
Scenario 2: 1 + stipend during leave of absence	$76,590	$76,590	—	—	—
Scenario 3: 1 + TRICARE for child	$304,910	$158,320	$553,576	$260,397	$189,613
Scenario 4: 2 + 3	$348,722	$202,132	$597,388	$304,209	$189,613
Scenario 5: 4 + additional stipend	$1,004,611	$393,123	$1,253,277	$495,200	$796,953
Scenario 6: 5 + child care subsidy	$1,823,907	$563,014	$2,072,574	$665,091	$1,645,332

SOURCES: Costs derived using data from DHA, 2021; DHA, 2022; DFAS, 2022; USNA, 2022; Department of the Army, U.S. Military Academy, 2021; Child Care Aware of America, undated; and estimates provided by DoD Comptroller's office.

NOTE: Costs in the year of birth are reported in 2022 dollars. Subsequent year costs are adjusted using a 3.9-percent medical inflation rate and 2.6-percent inflation rate for other expenses. Aggregates costs for three cadets or midshipmen who give birth and seven who father a child. Costs do not differ across the ten cases for cadets and midshipmen who enter the academy with a child in the final row. Costs are estimated for only the additional support costs modeled in each scenario and do not include the standard costs of education for each cadet or midshipman.

cases included in the aggregate. As in Table 4.3, we show the costs under profiles in which all ten cadets or midshipmen have a child in their first or last year at the academy to represent a range of potential costs.[11]

A similar pattern emerges in Table 4.4 as was shown in Table 4.3. Costs are approximately $33,000 under Scenario 1 and $77,000 under Scenario 2. The costs for Scenarios 1 and 2 are the same across the various time points (except for the profile in which all cadets enter with a child) because they cover only the costs of childbirth and one year of absence for the three cadets in the aggregation who give birth. For Scenario 3, which focuses only on the provision of health care for the pregnant cadet or midshipman and the child dependent, aggregate costs range between $158,000 and $305,000. When TRICARE is also included for a civilian

[11] Additional profiles are shown in Tables B.3 and B.4 in Appendix B. All aggregate profiles show total costs in a scenario in which ten cadets or midshipmen in a given cohort all become parents in the same year at the academy. Alternative profiles in which ten cadets or midshipmen become parents in different years (e.g., five become parents in their first year and five become parents in their third year), may be created by summing the individual totals shown in Tables B.1 or B.2.

co-parent, aggregate costs increase to as much as $554,000 for cadets and midshipmen who become parents in their first year. Under the scenario with the most supports provided (Scenario 6), aggregate costs range from $563,000 for ten cadets or midshipmen who become parents in their last year to $1.8 million for ten cadets or midshipmen who become parents in their first year. When TRICARE is also extended to a civilian co-parent, costs reach approximately $2 million for cadets and midshipmen who become parents in their first year. The costs for ten cadets and midshipmen who enter the academy with a child range from approximately $190,000 (Scenarios 3 and 4) to $1.6 million (Scenario 6).

Benchmarking Costs

As can be seen from the scenarios described here, the potential costs of this policy change could vary significantly, depending on which supports are determined to be in scope for the cadet or midshipman and their family. Costs are highest for cadets and midshipmen who give birth (rather than their co-parents), and costs increase when cadets and midshipmen become parents earlier in their tenure in the academy, meaning that more years of additional supports would be provided. In general, costs would be highest in the year of birth because of the additional health care costs for the birth and the newborn and would decline in subsequent years.

However, costs for the additional stipend and child care subsidy overall would exceed the cost of health care in a typical year. As can be seen from Table 4.2, one year of TRICARE coverage for one additional dependent is estimated to be approximately $4,500, compared with more than $14,000 for one year of additional stipend or more than $20,000 for one year of additional child care subsidy. TRICARE costs that occur only in the year of birth are approximately $17,600, a similar magnitude to one year of stipend or child care.

The question of whether these costs are large or small depends on the object of their comparison. Table 4.5 presents costs for four possible benchmarks: (1) the total cost of education for one cadet or midshipman who graduates after four years of education, (2) the total cost of four years of education for all cadets or midshipmen across the three MSAs in a graduating cohort, (3) the cost of four years of TRICARE for a single cadet or midshipman, and (4) the cost of four years of TRICARE for all cadets and midshipmen across the three MSAs in a graduating cohort. Our estimates are based on a graduating cohort of 3,600 cadets and midshipmen, a number consistent with recent demographic data provided by the MSAs.

We inflate the reported estimate of the total cost of education in FY 2022 as shown in Table 4.2 and total over four years to obtain an estimate of $378,365 as the cost of education for one cadet or midshipman.[12] Compared with this benchmark, the cost of providing additional supports to a single cadet or midshipman parent ranges between 3 percent (under Scenario 1) and 58 percent (Scenario 6 for a cadet or midshipman who gives birth in the first

[12] Note that Kamarck (2021) reports that the cost of a four-year education for a cadet or midshipman ranges between $400,000 and $600,000, but this range is based on estimates provided by the academies, and the methodology used to estimate the cost may vary. Some estimates in the higher end of this range could include general operating expenses for the academies, as well as direct education costs.

TABLE 4.5
Cost Benchmarks for Comparison

Benchmark for What?	Benchmark	Estimated Cost
Change in average per-graduate education costs (tuition, room, board, stipend, health care, etc.)	Cost of four years of MSA education for a single cadet or midshipman	$378,365
Change in average education costs for new cohort of military officers in a given year	Cost of four years of MSA education for all cadets and midshipmen across all three MSAs in a graduating cohort	$1.362 billion
Change in average per-graduate TRICARE costs	Cost of four years of TRICARE for a single cadet or midshipman	$20,027
Change in average TRICARE costs for new cohort of military officers in a given year	Cost of four years of TRICARE for all cadets and midshipmen across all three MSAs in a graduating cohort	$72 million

SOURCES: Costs derived using data from DHA, 2021; DHA, 2022; DFAS, 2022; and estimates provided by DoD Comptroller's office.

NOTE: Cost of education is inflated over four years using a 2.6-percent inflation rate. Medical costs are inflated using a 3.9-percent medical inflation rate.

year) of this cost.[13] If we aggregate the total cost of ten cadet or midshipman parents and compare with the aggregate cost of four years of education for a graduating cohort across all three MSAs, the aggregate costs in Table 4.4 range between 0.002 percent (Scenario 1) and 0.13 percent (Scenario 6 for ten cadets or midshipmen who become parents in the first year, excluding TRICARE costs for civilian co-parents) of the total cost of four years of education for all cadets and midshipmen in a graduating cohort.

To compare the implications for TRICARE costs only, we compare costs under Scenarios 1 and 3 with an estimate of four years of TRICARE costs for one cadet or midshipman and 3,600 cadets and midshipmen, using the annual estimate of TRICARE costs for a cadet or midshipman in Table 4.2 as the base. Additional TRICARE costs would range between 54 percent (Scenario 1) and 250 percent (Scenario 3, including TRICARE costs for a dependent co-parent) of total TRICARE costs for an individual cadet or midshipman over four years. Because the additional TRICARE costs reflect the costs of either childbirth or adding full coverage for an additional person over several years, it is not surprising that the costs are high relative to the base costs of providing TRICARE for one individual over four years. We estimate the aggregate additional TRICARE costs for ten cadet or midshipman parents would range between 0.05 percent (Scenario 1) and 0.77 percent (Scenario 3, including TRICARE costs for a dependent co-parent) of the cost of TRICARE for all cadets in a graduating cohort over their entire tenure at the MSAs.

As a result, the costs for a single cadet and midshipman may be sizable relative to the typical cost of education, depending on the supports offered and the timing of the birth. There is precedence for some of these additional costs—particularly, the costs of TRICARE

[13] We focus this discussion on scenarios and profiles with nonzero costs.

or a stipend during a leave of absence—to be provided under special circumstances. The AR on USMA states that cadets who are unable to perform their duties because of "physical disability or medical condition" can be granted a medical leave of absence of up to one year, and that "[c]adets on a medical leave of absence may continue to be paid in circumstances decided by the Commandant of Cadets."[14] We note this example to highlight that our benchmark estimate of the total cost of education for a single cadet or midshipman is itself an average based on a typical experience at the academy, but some atypical circumstances in fact already necessitate higher costs.

On the other hand, the numbers in the aggregate in our hypothetical scenario represent less than 1 percent of the total education costs or TRICARE costs for a graduating MSA cohort, if the number of cadet and midshipman parents is on the order of ten parents per cohort.

Implications for Recoupment

As discussed in Chapter 3, cadets and midshipmen in their last two years at the academy may be required to repay the costs of their education if they resign or are disenrolled but do not serve their active-duty commitment. Recoupment—whether and how much to recoup—is determined on a case-by-case basis, considering the circumstances of the disenrollment and reasons why the cadet or midshipman may not serve in active duty.[15] When the policy regarding parental rights changes, however, considerations for disenrollment and recoupment may also change for cadet or midshipman parents, since they would no longer be in violation of academy policy merely because they became parents.[16]

On one hand, cadet and midshipman parents who would have disenrolled may now stay at the academies, complete their education, and commission. If these parents would otherwise have been subject to recoupment, DoD will now pay the costs for the completion of their education (as well as possibly any additional parental supports); in return for these costs, DoD will commission another officer who would have disenrolled under the prior policy. To the extent that the change in policy retains additional cadet or midshipman parents who would have left in their first or second year (and thus not be required to serve in active duty or repay the costs of education), this would again convert funds that previously were forgone education costs into funds invested into another commissioned officer.

On the other hand, a cadet or midshipman parent may still decide to resign, but the new policy may change the determination of whether recoupment is required. If recoupment is not required in this case, DoD would forgo the funds that would have been recouped and may cover some initial costs for the parent or child if the cadet or midshipman does not disenroll

[14] AR 150-1, 2021, p. 43.

[15] DoDI 1322.22, 2015; Department of the Army, U.S. Military Academy, 2021; SECNAVINST 1531.4A, 2018; AR 150-1, 2021.

[16] For example, the May 2022 update to DAFI 36-3501 clarifies that it is no longer a policy violation for a cadet to remain at the academy after becoming pregnant or giving birth.

immediately. In this case, the costs of parenthood would increase by the amount of forgone recoupment. If the cadet or midshipman resigns in the first or second year, the forgone education costs would be the same as under current policy.

Given the specific nature of the circumstances surrounding recoupment and the fact that there are no exact data on cadets or midshipmen who became parents, it is impossible to determine exactly how many cadet or midshipman parents have had to pay back education costs after disenrolling because of parental rights issues in the past. However, data provided by the MSAs indicate that it is relatively rare for cadets or midshipmen to leave in their third or fourth year of school, be unable to fulfill their service commitment, and be required to repay their educational costs. According to data provided from the academies for this project, reported cases of recoupment for any reason ranged between zero and approximately 50 cases in a given academy per year over the past five years, with values of required recoupment ranging between $26,000 and $300,000.

Limitations

Many factors related to the specifics of the policy decisions to be made are unknown, and the data that are needed for a comprehensive cost analysis simply do not exist. Our analysis relies on assumptions and decisions based on the best available information at the time of our research, but these simplifications nevertheless yield several limitations to our analysis. First, the cost estimates do not include several programs and supports that could yield additional costs or savings to DoD and the cadet or midshipman. Most importantly, we do not model the costs of allowing a child to reside with the cadet or midshipman at the academy. As discussed, several other supports are provided to active-duty parents, and there could be future policy decisions to provide these supports to cadet or midshipman parents as well, including adoption benefits, the Exceptional Family Member Program, or new parent support programs. We also do not consider changes in cadet or midshipman tax liabilities or the impacts those changes could have on DoD payroll taxes.

We made some decisions to simplify the individual modeling scenarios, but the reality will likely be more complex. For example, we do not include the costs of one year of absence for cadets and midshipmen who father a child. If these parents also take a leave of absence at the time of their child's birth and are eligible to receive health care coverage or additional stipends during this time, that would further increase the cost. The per-unit, per-parent costs shown in Table 4.2 can be combined in any number of ways beyond the exact scenarios shown here to inform the costs under different policy decisions that we did not model.

Costs in the aggregated scenarios would be different if the ratio of cadets or midshipmen giving birth versus fathering a child is different from the 3-to-7 ratio used here. We also note that the aggregated total number of ten parents shown here is not based on any reported data of the total number of cadet or midshipman parents; these totals are unknown. Again, the per-parent total costs shown in Tables 4.3, B.1, and B.2 may be aggregated in any number of ways to inform the cost of a different total number of parents or a different mix of cadets and midshipmen who give birth or father a child at different points in their tenures at the academy.

Finally, some of the data for underlying cost inputs—particularly for TRICARE costs—are generic. For example, we were unable to obtain specific estimates of TRICARE costs differentiated by gender, age, or child dependent versus adult dependent. Although health care costs would vary for individuals based on these demographic characteristics, our analysis uses an average estimate for a family dependent irrespective of these demographic differences. We also assumed that cadet and midshipman costs would be equal to active-duty costs, though in reality utilization could be different, which would yield different costs. We derived the costs for pregnancy, child care, and postpartum and newborn care from aggregate totals reported in public reports. Actual costs could either increase or decrease the total cost estimates but would likely be of the same order of magnitude to the costs presented here. We also use the maximum child care subsidy amount to model child care, which could be an upper-bound estimate if cadets or midshipmen did not require the maximum subsidy amount or relied on unpaid care from family members or a co-parent who does not work.

Key Findings and Conclusions

The range of costs of allowing cadets and midshipmen to retain their parental rights is driven by the variety of options for supports that may be provided to the cadet or midshipman and their family, all of which represent policy decisions yet to be undertaken. In addition to presenting costs for a single cadet or midshipman parent under various support scenarios, we aggregate the cost to present total costs for ten cadet or midshipman parents. The true number of current cadet or midshipman parents is unknown, and the number of those who may become parents in the future may change as a result of the change in policy. Consequently, the assessment of costs here is informative for providing an order of magnitude of the total cost. We have designed our approach to offer examples of hypothetical scenarios and to provide building blocks for calculating the total cost in other ways beyond the specific scenarios modeled in this report. Although hypothetical, this exercise yields some important conclusions.

After the Year of Birth, the Costs of Child Care and Stipend Are Large Relative to the Cost of TRICARE for an Additional Dependent

The cost of TRICARE for a family dependent (either child or adult) is estimated to be approximately $4,500 per year, compared with approximately $14,000 per year for the additional stipend set at the current cadet or midshipman rate, or just over $20,000 per year for the maximum child care subsidy. Put another way, the cost of one year of child care subsidy is similar to the cost of providing TRICARE for a dependent over all four years that a cadet or midshipman may spend at the academy. In other words, TRICARE coverage would likely be the least expensive support for dependents of cadets or midshipmen—either child dependents or perhaps spouses if the marriage policy changes in the future. Furthermore, most health care costs would likely be absorbed in general DoD operating budgets rather than coming out of specific budgets of the MSAs.[17]

Although Additional Support Costs Could Appear Sizable for an Individual Cadet or Midshipman (Depending on the Supports Provided), They Could Be a Relatively Small Increase in Overall Costs for a Graduating MSA Cohort

Under the scenarios we considered, total costs for a single cadet or midshipman parent and their child range from $11,000 to approximately $220,000. Aggregated estimates for ten cadet and midshipman parents range from $33,000 to $1.8 million.[18] The final scenario we model includes TRICARE costs for the cadet or midshipman during pregnancy and childbirth, during the leave of absence, and for the child dependent over the cadet's or midshipman's remaining tenure at the academy. It also includes the regular stipend during a leave of absence, an additional stipend for the child, and the maximum child care subsidy.

If a cadet or midshipman were to give birth right after entering the academy and return after one year of absence to complete four years of study and training, the total costs of this scenario would be approximately 58 percent of the total cost of four years of education at the MSAs for a single cadet. If TRICARE costs were also included for the spouse, this total would increase to 65 percent of four years of education at the MSA. By this comparison, these supports would be a sizable benefit in the eyes of the cadet or midshipman and their family.

Although the actual number of cadets and midshipmen who become parents is unknown, the number is likely to be relatively small compared with the size of a total MSA cohort in a given year, even under the new policy. Under our notional example of ten cadet or midshipman parents in a given cohort, aggregate costs do not exceed 1 percent of four years of education costs for an entire graduating cohort or four years of TRICARE expenses, even under the scenario with the most supports that we modeled. Certainly, if a large number of cadets or midshipmen became parents, the costs would be larger.

Finally, some of these costs—particularly the costs of TRICARE or stipends during a leave of absence—are currently covered under unique circumstances to cadets or midshipmen with unexpected medical issues or other life emergencies. We highlight this provision because our benchmark estimate of the total cost of education for a single cadet or midshipman is itself an average based on a typical experience at the academy, but some unique circumstances already necessitate higher costs.

---

17 Office of the Under Secretary of Defense, Comptroller, *Defense Health Program Operation and Maintenance, Defense-Wide Fiscal Year (FY) 2022 Budget Estimates Introductory Statement*, U.S. Department of Defense, 2022a.

18 Note that these ranges exclude scenarios with zero cost and scenarios in which civilian partners receive TRICARE.

Additional Supports Not Modeled May Either Increase the Cost or Yield Savings

Several additional supports were not included in our model. We did not factor in changes in costs if housing policies were to change. We also did not include the costs of other new parent support programs, Exceptional Family Member programs, or adoption benefits. We are not aware of discussions to extend these supports to cadet and midshipman parents at this time, but all of them could be potential policy changes to be considered. Offering a housing benefit or expanding family housing at the MSA would likely have significant costs. On the other hand, the cost of extending other benefits to cadet or midshipman parents would likely be relatively small because the fixed cost for standing up these programs has already been incurred. If these additional supports help a cadet or midshipman parent remain at the academy and commission, they could offer savings relative to the cost of education that would have been lost if a cadet or midshipman resigns. Additional savings may come from changes in tax liability for the cadet or DoD, lowering the total cost of providing these additional supports.

CHAPTER 5

Recommendations for Military Policy Alignment, Implementation, and Assessment

The FY 2022 NDAA required changes to DoD regulations to provide cadets and midshipmen who become biological parents while enrolled at an MSA the option to retain their parental rights, "consistent with [their] individual and academic responsibilities."[1] If no additional pay or benefits are available to help cadets and midshipmen who become parents, some will surely face difficulties meeting their children's needs while successfully completing the rigorous demands of their MSA professional and academic development. As a result, we focus our recommendations on structuring policy changes and leveraging existing support structures to help cadet and midshipman parents balance parenthood and succeed as military officers.

DoD should adopt policy options for cadet and midshipman parents that are consistent with its policies for other active-duty personnel, leveraging the strengths of its Military Family Readiness System. Additional pay, benefits, and program and service supports from the Military Family Readiness System could be offered to help ensure cadet and midshipman health, well-being, and ability to focus on professional and academic responsibilities. Additional resources could also help address inequities, as not all cadets and midshipmen will have the resources or family support systems that can financially provide for them and their child. These military supports could be structured in a way that attracts and retains quality officers and improves DoD's return on investment. For example, additional supports for parenthood could be linked to an earlier service commitment (i.e., in the first or second year at the academy) or a longer service obligation after graduation. If cadet or midshipman parents are unable or unwilling to remain at the academies—either on a temporary basis around the birth of a child or permanently—policies could be structured to facilitate a transition to other programs to enhance retention. DoD could assist cadet or midshipman parents in transitioning to a suitable ROTC program and securing a scholarship, which could help keep high-quality candidates in the officer pipeline while providing greater flexibility for exercising parental rights. Another option is that DoD could establish a program to allow cadets and midshipmen who are becoming parents to move to enlisted status for a set period,

[1] Public Law 117-81, Section 559A, 2021.

during which they could earn better pay and receive full benefits for themselves and their child and then either request academy readmission or fulfill an enlisted term of service.[2]

DoD, the military departments, and the MSAs should create detailed policies on MSA practices related to pregnancy, childbirth, and postpartum care. Senior leader guidance could help prevent inconsistency and dangerous or discriminatory actions. The update to DoDI 1322.22 on the service academies will provide higher-level guidance on physical fitness requirements. More local guidance will be needed to manage various issues, such as logistics for prenatal medical appointments; permissions for fathers to attend childbirth; and accommodations for pregnancy and postpartum needs, such as morning sickness and lactation. The MSAs could coordinate on some standardization across their policies, but certain aspects may need to be tailored to each particular location (e.g., depending on the availability of certain resources on or near the campus) or the particular needs of an individual.

In the short term, while other policy options might be under development, DoD should take some basic steps to ensure the health and well-being of cadets and midshipmen who are becoming parents and their children. While DoD is considering myriad policy questions surrounding parental rights, DoD could decide, in the short term, to provide medical or administrative leave with health care spanning a cadet's or midshipman's period of pregnancy, childbirth, and postpartum care, as well as health care coverage for the child. It seems DoD could make this change; cadets and midshipmen are categorized as active-duty personnel in some respects, and there appears to be no language in the U.S. Code prohibiting their children from receiving health care similar to that of children of other active-duty personnel. However, Section 559A of the FY 2022 NDAA did not explicitly address this issue, and the law does at times call out cadets and midshipmen as exceptions to active-duty personnel entitlements,[3] so additional legislative clarity may be needed to confirm or provide eligibility.

DoD and the MSAs should develop and implement plans to ensure that applicants as well as cadets and midshipmen understand new policies regarding their parental rights and responsibilities. Cadets and midshipmen should be informed of any local, state, federal, or military resources available to support cadet and midshipman parents; options for continuing or discontinuing their enrollment and recoupment; and applicable associated policies (e.g., leave policies or policies regarding pregnancy). The implementation of any new policies should include direct communication with students and a publicized repository of such information that is easily accessible to cadets and midshipmen.

DoD should conduct or support further qualitative research needed to evaluate possible changes to housing, child development centers, and cadet and midshipman privileges. These policy options will require additional study to fully appreciate their implications. Changes might be intended to support the health and well-being of cadets and midshipmen and their families, but the same changes could also have an impact on cadets' and midship-

[2] The MSAs' mentorship programs discussed in Chapter 3 could serve as a model for this enlisted option.

[3] As one example, U.S. Code, Title 10, Section 702(c) states that Sections 701, 703, and 704 regarding personnel leave do not apply to academy cadets or midshipmen.

men's studies and their professionalization, fellow students, and availability of housing and child care to MSA faculty and staff. Any proposed changes to allow cadets and midshipmen who are parents to use MSA family housing or child development centers or to have other privileges that their peers do not have (e.g., have a car, miss activities, leave campus to visit their child) need to be thoroughly explored and carefully considered before being adopted.

While new and revised policies are being established, DoD and the MSAs should collect, monitor, and analyze data on the parenthood status of cadets and midshipmen and the potential impacts of the policy changes. Data on parenthood status of cadets and midshipmen should be used to better understand the demographic characteristics of this subgroup and examine patterns related to their enrollment, performance, and retention. Analyses of such data also might be useful to identify potential signs of disparate impact or indicators that additional supports or guidance may be needed. Finally, such data could provide insight on reasons for resignation or disenrollment. To refine the new policies and practices and adapt to evolving trends, MSA leadership should review reports of this information at least annually, with the goal of improving the policies and practices that support the integration and success of the parents, as well as the welfare of the parents and their families.

DoD should also require the MSAs to collect and analyze data and submit an assessment of the implementation of parental rights–related policy changes on the MSAs' ability to execute their missions and any associated impacts to cadet and midshipman culture, morale, and quality of life. Reports should be submitted at certain milestones after implementation of the Secretary of Defense's new policy (e.g., the one-, three-, and five-year points) to allow time for the academies to accumulate experience and data regarding implementation and to provide a mechanism for DoD to assess potential impact and any need for additional guidance or policy refinements.

Table 5.1 provides an overview of our recommendations and shows that, with the exception of health care benefits, these actions will involve policy changes and implementation activities across organizations.

TABLE 5.1

Recommendations Overview, by Responsible Organizations

Recommendation	Responsible Organizations OSD	Military Departments	MSAs
Family readiness supports aligned with those for other active-duty personnel	X	X	X
Leave of absence for cadet/midshipman pregnancy, childbirth, postpartum care	X	X	X
Health care coverage for child	X		
Health care during cadet/midshipman absence for pregnancy, childbirth, postpartum care	X		
Awareness of policy changes, rights, responsibilities	X	X	X
Further investigation of family housing and child development center options	X	X	X
Data collection, monitoring, analysis to inform and improve new policies	X	X	X

APPENDIX A

Military Policy Review Search Approach

This appendix provides additional methodological details on our approach to the military policy review presented in Chapter 3. We used multiple strategies to identify potentially relevant policies at the hierarchical levels of OSD, the military departments, and local MSAs. This appendix lists the repositories we searched and explains how the searches were conducted.

We conducted keyword searches for published policies located in DoD and military department online repositories. We searched for DoD instructions, manuals, directives, and directive-type memoranda in the Washington Headquarters Services Issuances repository. We searched for military department and service policies through the Department of the Air Force E-Publishing repository, the Department of the Army Publishing Directorate repository, and the Department of the Navy Issuances repository.

Our search terms included the following variations of keywords, co-occurring words that do not have to appear side by side (indicated by "AND"), and key phrases (indicated by quotation marks):

- academies, academy
- appoint, appointment
- cadet
- child custody
- child care
- child support
- convenience
- commission, commissioning
- custody AND child, custody AND children, custody AND dependent
- dependent
- disenroll, disenrollment
- "disqualifying conditions"
- family
- hardship AND officer
- "leave of absence," "leaves of absence"
- "medical disqualification"
- "medical leave"
- "medical standards"
- midshipman, midshipmen

- "military parental leave"
- "Officer Candidate School," "Officer Training School"
- parent, parental, parenthood
- pregnancy, pregnant
- recoup, recoupment
- "Reserve Officer Training Corps," ROTC
- resign, resignation
- separation AND officer
- "service obligation" AND officer.

From the results of these searches, we mined the references for possible leads to other relevant policies. We also noted the policies raised in the OSD working group on cadet and midshipman parental rights. Furthermore, we received suggestions from our sponsor and representatives from the military departments and MSAs.

As our search and review process progressed, we developed nine categories for grouping the policy issues related to cadet and midshipman parental rights. The categories helped us refine our search terms, revealed what topics were missing from our search, and ultimately were used to code the policies for our analysis. The nine categories are

- admissions criteria and processes
- pregnancy (management of the physical and medical aspects)
- leaves of absence
- family/dependent-related care, pay, and benefits
- legal support services available to cadets and midshipmen (e.g., for advice or support with family court issues)
- disenrollment/resignation
- reimbursement/recoupment of educational expenses for those who resign or are disenrolled
- service obligations for MSA graduates and nongraduates
- officer commissioning standards.

We began our analysis by organizing excerpts of the relevant portion of the policy by category. Then, we analyzed the policy excerpts to identify

- language that will need to be changed to comply with the FY 2022 NDAA requirement
- language that points to a policy decision to be made
- language that could serve as an example for how policies could be revised
- consistency by hierarchical level: U.S. Code, OSD, military department, MSA
- similarities and differences across military departments and MSAs.

We further synthesized this information into the results presented in Chapter 3.

APPENDIX B

Additional Cost Results

Chapter 4 presents cost estimates for select profiles of cadets and midshipmen under each of the cost scenarios. The profiles vary based on the years remaining at the academy, whether the cadet or midshipman gives birth while enrolled at the academy, whether the cadet or midshipman enters the academy with a child, and whether TRICARE costs are included for a civilian spouse. In Chapter 4, we present results for cadets and midshipmen with one and four years remaining at the academy to highlight the variety of potential costs. In Tables B.1 through B.4, we provide cost estimates for all potential profiles.

TABLE B.1

Cost of Additional Supports for One Cadet or Midshipman Parent, Under Various Scenarios

Cadet/Midshipman Gives Birth?	Cadet/Midshipman Enters Academy with a Child?	Years Remaining at the Academy	Scenario					
			1	2	3	4	5	6
Yes	No	1	$10,926	$25,530	$26,733	$41,337	$70,924	$91,855
Yes	No	2	$10,926	$25,530	$31,560	$46,164	$91,125	$133,530
Yes	No	3	$10,926	$25,530	$36,576	$51,180	$111,914	$176,352
Yes	No	4	$10,926	$25,530	$41,787	$56,391	$133,308	$220,352
No	No	1	—	—	$11,160	$11,160	$25,764	$41,064
No	No	2	—	—	$15,807	$15,807	$45,394	$81,625
No	No	3	—	—	$20,634	$20,634	$65,595	$123,300
No	No	4	—	—	$25,650	$25,650	$86,384	$166,122
No	Yes	4	—	—	$18,961	$18,961	$79,695	$164,533

SOURCE: Costs derived using data from DHA, 2021; DHA, 2022; DFAS, 2022; USNA, 2022; Department of the Army, U.S. Military Academy, 2021; Child Care Aware of America, undated; and estimates provided by DoD Comptroller's office.

NOTE: Costs in the year of birth are reported in 2022 dollars. Subsequent year costs are adjusted using a 3.9-percent medical inflation rate and 2.6-percent inflation rate for other expenses.

TABLE B.2

Cost of Additional Supports for One Cadet or Midshipman Parent, Under Various Scenarios, Including the Cost of TRICARE for a Civilian Co-Parent Dependent

Cadet/ Midshipman Gives Birth?	Cadet/ Midshipman Enters Academy with a Child?	Years Remaining at the Academy	Scenario			
			3	4	5	6
Yes	No	1	$35,851	$50,455	$80,042	$100,973
Yes	No	2	$45,506	$60,110	$105,071	$147,476
Yes	No	3	$55,537	$70,141	$130,875	$195,313
Yes	No	4	$65,960	$80,564	$157,481	$244,525
No	No	1	$21,835	$21,835	$36,439	$51,739
No	No	2	$31,127	$31,127	$60,715	$96,946
No	No	3	$40,782	$40,782	$85,743	$143,448
No	No	4	$50,814	$50,814	$111,548	$191,286
No	Yes	4	$37,923	$37,923	$98,657	$183,495

SOURCE: Costs derived using data from DHA, 2021; DHA, 2022; DFAS, 2022; USNA, 2022; Department of the Army, U.S. Military Academy, 2021; Child Care Aware of America, undated; and estimates provided by DoD Comptroller's office.

NOTE: Costs in the year of birth are reported in 2022 dollars. Subsequent year costs are adjusted using a 3.9-percent medical inflation rate and 2.6-percent inflation rate for other expenses. TRICARE costs for the civilian co-parent vary depending on whether the cadet or midshipman gives birth or the civilian co-parent does. Costs are estimated only for the additional support costs modeled in each scenario and do not include the standard costs of education for each cadet or midshipman.

TABLE B.3

Aggregated Cost of Additional Supports for Ten Cadet or Midshipman Parents, Under Various Scenarios

Years Remaining at the Academy	Scenario					
	1	2	3	4	5	6
1	$32,778	$76,590	$158,320	$202,132	$393,123	$563,014
2	$32,778	$76,590	$205,326	$249,138	$591,135	$971,962
3	$32,778	$76,590	$254,165	$297,977	$794,906	$1,392,155
4	$32,778	$76,590	$304,910	$348,722	$1,004,611	$1,823,907
4 (enters with a child)	—	—	$189,613	$189,613	$796,953	$1,645,332

SOURCE: Costs derived using data from DHA, 2021; DHA, 2022; DFAS, 2022; USNA, 2022; Department of the Army, U.S. Military Academy, 2021; Child Care Aware of America, undated; and estimates provided by DoD Comptroller's office.

NOTE: Costs in the year of birth are reported in 2022 dollars. Subsequent year costs are adjusted using a 3.9-percent medical inflation rate and 2.6-percent inflation rate for other expenses. Aggregates costs for three cadets or midshipmen who give birth and seven who have co-parents give birth. Costs do not differ across the ten cases for cadets and midshipmen who enter the academy with a child in the final row. Costs are estimated only for the additional support costs modeled in each scenario and do not include the standard costs of education for each cadet or midshipman.

TABLE B.4

Aggregated Cost of Additional Supports for Ten Cadet or Midshipman Parents, Under Various Scenarios, Including the Cost of TRICARE for a Civilian Co-Parent Dependent

Years Remaining at the Academy	Scenario			
	3	4	5	6
1	$260,397	$304,209	$495,200	$665,091
2	$354,409	$398,221	$740,218	$1,121,046
3	$452,088	$495,900	$992,829	$1,590,077
4	$553,576	$597,388	$1,253,277	$2,072,574
4 (enters with a child)	$379,227	$379,227	$986,566	$1,834,945

SOURCE: Costs derived using data from DHA, 2021; DHA, 2022; DFAS, 2022; USNA, 2022; Department of the Army, U.S. Military Academy, 2021; Child Care Aware of America, undated; and estimates provided by DoD Comptroller's office.

NOTE: Costs in the year of birth are reported in 2022 dollars. Subsequent year costs are adjusted using a 3.9-percent medical inflation rate and 2.6-percent inflation rate for other expenses. Aggregates costs for three cadets or midshipmen who give birth and seven who have co-parents give birth. TRICARE costs for the civilian co-parent vary depending on whether the cadet or midshipman gives birth or the civilian co-parent does. Costs do not differ across the ten cases for cadets and midshipmen who enter the academy with a child in the final row. Costs are estimated only for the additional support costs modeled in each scenario and do not include the standard costs of education for each cadet or midshipman.

Abbreviations

AR	Army Regulation
ASFA	Adoption and Safe Families Act
COMDTMIDNINST	Commandant of Midshipmen Instruction
DAFI	Department of the Air Force Instruction
DFAS	Defense Finance and Accounting Service
DHA	Defense Health Agency
DoD	U.S. Department of Defense
DoDI	Department of Defense Instruction
FY	fiscal year
MSA	military service academy
NDAA	National Defense Authorization Act
OSD	Office of the Secretary of Defense
ROTC	Reserve Officers' Training Corps
SCRA	Servicemembers Civil Relief Act
SECNAVINST	Secretary of the Navy Instruction
TPR	termination of parental rights
UCCJEA	Uniform Child Custody Justification and Enforcement Act
UIFSA	Uniform Interstate Family Support Act
USAFA	U.S. Air Force Academy
USAFAI	U.S. Air Force Academy Instruction
USMA	U.S. Military Academy
USNA	U.S. Naval Academy

Bibliography

Air Force Cadet Wing Instruction 36-3501, *Cadet Standards and Duties*, U.S. Air Force Academy, August 12, 2020.

Air Force Cadet Wing Instruction 36-3501, *Cadet Standards and Duties*, U.S. Air Force Academy, August 9, 2021.

Air Force Information Management Tool 357, *Family Care Certification*, Department of the Air Force, undated.

Air Force Instruction 36-2012, *Record of Disenrollment from Officer Candidate-Type Training*, Department of the Air Force, March 7, 2019.

Air Force Manual 41-210, *TRICARE Operations and Patient Administration*, Department of the Air Force, September 10, 2019.

Air Force ROTC Instruction 36-2011, Vol. 3, *Cadet Operations*, Air Force Reserve Officer Training Corps, December 30, 2020.

Alaska Statutes, Title 47, Welfare, Social Services, and Institutions; Chapter 10, Children in Need of Aid; Article 1, Children's Proceedings; Section 47.10.013, Abandonment, 2022.

AR—*See* Army Regulation.

Army Directive 2022-06, *Parenthood, Pregnancy, and Postpartum*, Department of the Army, April 19, 2022.

Army Regulation 27-3, *The Army Legal Assistance Program*, Department of the Army, March 26, 2020.

Army Regulation 40-501, *Standards of Medical Fitness*, Department of the Army, June 27, 2019.

Army Regulation 135-210, *Army National Guard and Reserve: Order to Active Duty as Individuals for Other Than a Presidential Reserve Call-Up, Partial or Full Mobilization*, Department of the Army, September 17, 2019.

Army Regulation 140-10, *Army Reserve: Assignments, Attachments, Details, and Transfers*, Department of the Army, July 16, 2021.

Army Regulation 145-1, *Reserve Officers' Training Corps: Senior Reserve Officers' Training Corps Program: Organization, Administration, and Training*, Department of the Army, July 22, 1996, Rapid Action Revision Issue Date September 6, 2011.

Army Regulation 150-1, *United States Military Academy: Organization, Administration, and Operation*, Department of the Army, January 12, 2021.

Army Regulation 350-100, *Officer Active Duty Service Obligations*, Department of the Army, September 26, 2017.

Army Regulation 600-4, *Remission or Cancellation of Indebtedness*, Department of the Army, April 20, 2021.

Army Regulation 600-20, *Army Command Policy*, Department of the Army, July 24, 2020.

Army Regulation 608-10, *Child Development Services*, Department of the Army, May 11, 2017.

Army Regulation 608-99, *Family Support, Child Custody, and Parentage*, Department of the Army, November 13, 2020.

Army Regulation 638-2, *Army Mortuary Affairs Program*, Department of the Army, July 13, 2021.

Asch, Beth J., Patricia K. Tong, Lisa Berdie, and Michael G. Mattock, *Evaluation of Flexible Spending Accounts for Active-Duty Service Members,* RAND Corporation, RR-A1553-1, 2022. As of May 30, 2022:
https://www.rand.org/pubs/research_reports/RRA1553-1.html

Asch, Beth J., and John D. Winkler, *Ensuring Language Capability in the Intelligence Community: What Factors Affect the Best Mix of Military, Civilians, and Contractors?* RAND Corporation, TR-1284-ODNI, 2013. As of August 25, 2022:
https://www.rand.org/pubs/technical_reports/TR1284.html

CC—*See* U.S. Commandant of Cadets Policy Memorandum Number.

Child Care Aware of America, "DoD Fee Assistance," webpage, undated. As of November 15, 2022:
https://www.childcareaware.org/fee-assistancerespite/dod-families/dod-fee-assistance

Child Welfare Information Gateway, "Guardianship," webpage, undated-a. As of November 28, 2022:
https://www.childwelfare.gov/topics/permanency/guardianship/

Child Welfare Information Gateway, "Kinship Care," webpage, undated-b. As of December 3, 2022:
https://www.childwelfare.gov/topics/outofhome/kinship/

Child Welfare Information Gateway, *Determining the Best Interests of the Child*, U.S. Department of Health and Human Services, Administration for Children and Families, Children's Bureau, 2020.

Child Welfare Information Gateway, *Grounds for Involuntary Termination of Parental Rights*, U.S. Department of Health and Human Services, Administration for Children and Families, Children's Bureau, 2021.

Child Welfare Information Gateway, *Kinship Care and the Child Welfare System*, U.S. Department of Health and Human Services, Administration for Children and Families, Children's Bureau, May 2022.

Clever, Molly, and David R. Segal, "The Demographics of Military Children and Families," *Future of Children*, Vol. 23, No. 2, 2013.

Commandant of Midshipmen Instruction 1531.2B, *Procedures and Instructions in Cases of Midshipman Pregnancy/Parenthood/Dependency*, U.S. Naval Academy, April 6, 2015.

Commandant of Midshipmen Instruction 1600.2J, *Midshipmen Aptitude for Commissioning System*, U.S. Naval Academy, August 3, 2018.

COMDTMIDNINST—*See* Commandant of Midshipmen Instruction.

Consolidated Laws of New York; Chapter 14, Domestic Relations, September 22, 2014.

DAFI—*See* Department of the Air Force Instruction.

Defense Finance and Accounting Service, "Monthly Rates of Basic Pay—Effective January 1, 2022," U.S. Department of Defense, 2022. As of November 15, 2022:
https://www.dfas.mil/militarymembers/payentitlements/Pay-Tables/Basic-Pay/EM/2022

Defense Health Agency, *Evaluation of the TRICARE Program: Fiscal Year 2021 Report to Congress: Access, Cost, and Quality Data Through Fiscal Year 2020*, U.S. Department of Defense, February 26, 2021.

Defense Health Agency, *Evaluation of the TRICARE Program: Fiscal Year 2022 Report to Congress: Access, Cost, and Quality Data Through Fiscal Year 2021*, U.S. Department of Defense, February 28, 2022.

Defense Manpower Data Center, "Appendix B: Active Component Enlisted Accessions, Enlisted Force, Officer Accessions, and Officer Corps Tables," dataset, undated-a.

Defense Manpower Data Center, "Appendix D: Historical Data Tables," dataset, undated-b.

Defense Travel System, U.S. Department of Defense, "2021 Non-Locality BAH Rates," dataset, January 2021.

Department of Defense Directive-Type Memorandum 22-004, *Reserve Component Maternity Leave Program*, U.S. Department of Defense, June 9, 2022.

Department of Defense Directive-Type Memorandum 23-001, *Expansion of the Military Parental Leave Program*, U.S. Department of Defense, January 4, 2023.

Department of Defense Financial Management Regulation 7000.14-R, Vol. 7A, *Military Pay Policy—Active Duty and Reserve Pay*, Ch. 2, *Repayment of Unearned Portion of Bonuses and Other Benefits*, Under Secretary of Defense (Comptroller), May 2020.

Department of Defense Instruction 1120.11, *Programming and Accounting for Active Component (AC) Military Manpower*, U.S. Department of Defense, March 17, 2015.

Department of Defense Instruction 1215.08, *Senior Reserve Officers' Training Corps (ROTC) Programs*, U.S. Department of Defense, January 19, 2017, change 1, March 7, 2018.

Department of Defense Instruction 1322.22, *Service Academies*, U.S. Department of Defense, September 24, 2015.

Department of Defense Instruction 1327.06, *Leave and Liberty Policy and Procedures*, U.S. Department of Defense, June 16, 2009, change 4, January 15, 2021.

Department of Defense Instruction 1340.24, *Family Separation Allowance (FSA)*, U.S. Department of Defense, September 17, 2009.

Department of Defense Instruction 1341.11, *Family Subsistence Supplemental Allowance (FSSA) Program*, U.S. Department of Defense, March 4, 2008.

Department of Defense Instruction 1342.19, *Family Care Plans*, U.S. Department of Defense, May 7, 2010, change 1, November 30, 2017.

Department of Defense Instruction 1342.22, *Military Family Readiness*, U.S. Department of Defense, August 5, 2021.

Department of Defense Instruction 6130.03, Vol. 1, *Medical Standards for Military Service: Appointment, Enlistment, or Induction*, U.S. Department of Defense, May 6, 2018, change 4, November 16, 2022.

Department of Defense Manual 1000.13, Vol. 2, *DoD Identification (ID) Cards: Benefits for Members of the Uniformed Services, Their Dependents, and Other Eligible Individuals*, U.S. Department of Defense, January 23, 2014, change 1, August 5, 2020.

Department of the Air Force, "Personnel Services Delivery Guide: Family Care Plan," September 8, 2011.

Department of the Air Force Guidance Memorandum 2022-01 to DAFI 36-3003, *Military Leave Program*, Department of the Air Force, April 6, 2022.

Department of the Air Force Guidance Memorandum 2022-01 to DAFI 36-3003, *Military Leave Program*, Department of the Air Force, January 5, 2023a.

Department of the Air Force Guidance Memorandum 2022-01 to DAFI 36-3003, *Military Leave Program*, Department of the Air Force, March 30, 2023b.

Department of the Air Force Guidance Memorandum to Department of the Air Force Manual 36-2032, *Military Recruiting and Accessions*, Department of the Air Force, April 19, 2022.

Department of the Air Force Instruction 36-3501, *United States Air Force Academy Operations*, Department of the Air Force, May 9, 2022.

Department of the Air Force Manual 36-2905, *Department of the Air Force Physical Fitness Program*, Department of the Air Force, April 21, 2022.

Department of the Army, U.S. Military Academy, "Cadet Budget, Academic Year 2021–2022," August 2021.

DFAS—*See* Defense Finance and Accounting Service.

DHA—*See* Defense Health Agency.

DoDI—*See* Department of Defense Instruction.

Elrod, Linda D., "The Federalization of Family Law," *Human Rights Magazine*, Vol. 36, No. 3, Summer 2009.

Field Manual 7-22, *Holistic Health and Fitness*, Department of the Army, October 2020.

Freeland, Justin P., "All The Process That Is Due: An Article on Cadet Disenrollments from the United States Military Academy and the Army Reserve Officers' Training Corps," *Army Lawyer*, September 2015.

FY 2022 NDAA—*See* Public Law 117-81.

Garner, Bryan A., ed., *A Handbook of Family Law Terms*, West Group, 2001.

Generations United, "Adoption and Guardianship for Children in Kinship Foster Care: National Comparison Chart," 2021.

Goldrick-Rab, Sara, and Kia Sorensen, "Unmarried Parents in College," *Future of Children*, Vol. 20, No. 2, Fall 2010.

Hanser, Lawrence M., and Mustafa Oguz, *United States Service Academy Admissions: Selecting for Success at the Military Academy/West Point and as an Officer*, RAND Corporation, RR-723-OSD, 2015. As of July 23, 2022:
https://www.rand.org/pubs/research_reports/RR723.html

Hardison, Chaitra M., Susan Burkhauser, and Lawrence M. Hanser, *United States Service Academy Admissions: Selecting for Success at the Air Force Academy and as an Officer*, RAND Corporation, RR-744-OSD, 2016. As of July 24, 2022:
https://www.rand.org/pubs/research_reports/RR744.html

Hartman, Mike, *Modernizing Minor Guardianship in State Courts*, National Conference of State Legislatures, June 2022.

Hogan, Paul F., and Rita Furst Seifert, "Marriage and the Military: Evidence That Those Who Serve Marry Earlier and Divorce Earlier," *Armed Forces & Society*, Vol. 36, No. 3, April 2010.

Kamarck, Kristy N., *Defense Primer: Military Service Academies*, Congressional Research Service, IF11788, December 9, 2021.

Kizer, Kenneth W., and Suzanne Le Menestrel, eds., *Strengthening the Military Family Readiness System for a Changing American Society*, National Academies Press, 2019.

MacDonald, Kris, "A Review of the Literature: The Needs of Nontraditional Students in Postsecondary Education," *Strategic Enrollment Management Quarterly*, Vol. 5, No. 4, January 2018.

Manpower Information System Support Activity, "Family Care Plan (FCP): User Role," briefing, U.S. Marine Corps, January 16, 2018.

Marine Corps Order 1740.13C, *Family Care Plans*, U.S. Marine Corps, March 25, 2013.

Maryland Code, Family Law Article, 2022.

Military OneSource, "Military Child Care Programs," webpage, undated. As of May 11, 2023: https://www.militaryonesource.mil/benefits/military-child-care-programs/

Military Personnel Manual 1910-124, Ch. 72, *Separation by Reason of Convenience of the Government—Parenthood (Failure to Maintain Current Family Care Plan)*, Navy Personnel Command, December 29, 2020.

Minnesota Statutes, Chapter 260C, Child Protection, Section 260C.301, Termination of Parental Rights, 2022.

Myers, John E. B., *Family Law in a Nutshell*, 7th ed., West Publishing, 2019.

National Conference of State Legislatures, "Reinstatement of Parental Rights State Statute Summary," January 17, 2020.

Navy Personnel (NAVPERS) 1740.6, *Department of the Navy Family Care Certificate*, Department of the Navy, February 2011.

Navy Personnel (NAVPERS) 1740/7, "Family Care Plan Arrangements," Department of the Navy, February 2011.

Office of Child Support Enforcement, *Applicability of the Full Faith and Credit for Child Support Orders Act to States and Tribes*, Action Transmittal 02-03, May 28, 2002, current as of September 24, 2021.

Office of the Chief of Naval Operations Instruction 1000.26B, *Fulfilling the Military Service Obligation*, U.S. Navy, June 1, 2016.

Office of the Chief of Naval Operations Instruction 1420.1B, *Enlisted to Officer Commissioning Programs Application Administrative Manual*, U.S. Navy, December 14, 2009.

Office of the Chief of Naval Operations Instruction 1531.2C, *The Naval Academy Information Program (NAIP)*, U.S. Navy, December 3, 2006.

Office of the Chief of Naval Operations Instruction 1740.4E, *U.S. Navy Family Care Policy*, U.S. Navy, October 5, 2017.

Office of the Chief of Naval Operations Instruction 1700.9E, *Child and Youth Program*, U.S. Navy, July 10, 2008, change 1, September 24, 2012.

Office of the Chief of Naval Operations Instruction 1900.4A, *Separation Pay for Involuntary Separation from Active Duty*, U.S. Navy, February 19, 2019.

Office of the Chief of Naval Operations Instruction 5450.330B, *Missions, Functions, and Tasks of the United States Naval Academy, Annapolis, Maryland*, U.S. Navy, November 6, 2017.

Office of the Chief of Naval Operations Instruction 6000.1D, *Navy Guidelines Concerning Pregnancy and Parenthood*, U.S. Navy, March 12, 2018.

Office of the Under Secretary of Defense, Comptroller, "Department of Defense (DoD) Reimbursable Rate for Service Academies' Foreign Cadet and Midshipman for Academic Year 2021/2022," budget, October 18, 2021.

Office of the Under Secretary of Defense, Comptroller, *Defense Health Program Operation and Maintenance, Defense-Wide Fiscal Year (FY) 2022 Budget Estimates Introductory Statement*, U.S. U.S. Department of Defense, 2022a.

Office of the Under Secretary of Defense, Comptroller, *National Defense Budget Estimates for FY 2023*, U.S. Department of Defense, July 2022b.

People's Law Library of Maryland, "Kinship Care," webpage, undated. As of February 1, 2022: https://www.peoples-law.org/cat/family-law/kinship-care

People's Law Library of Maryland, "Child Custody in Maryland," webpage, January 17, 2022a. As of May 30, 2022:
https://www.peoples-law.org/child-custody-maryland

People's Law Library of Maryland, "Guardianship of a Minor—Frequently Asked Questions," webpage, January 17, 2022b. As of May 30, 2022:
https://www.peoples-law.org/guardianship-minor-frequently-asked-questions

Public Law 103-383, Full Faith and Credit for Child Support Orders Act, October 20, 1994.

Public Law 105-89, Adoption and Safe Families Act of 1997, November 19, 1997.

Public Law 113-183, Preventing Sex Trafficking and Strengthening Families Act of 2014, September 29, 2014.

Public Law 117-81, National Defense Authorization Act for Fiscal Year 2022, December 27, 2021.

Revised Statutes of Nebraska, Chapter 43, Infants and Juveniles; Article 2, Juvenile Code; Section 43-292, Termination of Parental Rights; Grounds, 2022.

Scheinkman, Alan D., and Matthew W. Lisle, "Child Custody and Visitation," Section 28.02, Elements of the Proceeding, *Child Custody and Visitation Law and Practice*, Matthew Bender & Co., Release 77, October 2022.

SECNAVINST—*See* Secretary of the Navy Instruction.

Secretary of the Navy Instruction 1000.10B, *Department of the Navy (DON) Policy on Parenthood and Pregnancy*, Department of the Navy, January 16, 2019.

Secretary of the Navy Instruction 1531.2D, *United States Naval Academy Curriculum and Admissions Policy*, Department of the Navy, November 27, 2018.

Secretary of the Navy Instruction 1531.4A, *U.S. Naval Academy Midshipmen Disenrollment*, Department of the Navy, November 28, 2018.

Secretary of the Navy Instruction 5820.9B, *Compliance with Court Orders by Department of the Navy Members, Employees, and Family Members Outside the United States*, Department of the Navy, May 2, 2019.

South Dakota Codified Laws, Title 26, Minors; Chapter 26-8A, Protection of Children from Abuse or Neglect; Section 26-8A.1, Termination of Parental Rights—Good Cause Considerations, 2022.

Taniguchi, Hiromi, and Gayle Kaufman, "Degree Completion Among Nontraditional College Students," *Social Science Quarterly*, Vol. 86, No. 4, December 2005.

Thurgood Marshall State Law Library, homepage, undated. As of June 21, 2023:
https://peoples-law.org

Uniform Law Commission, "About Us," webpage, undated-a. As of November 28, 2022: http://uniformlaws.org/aboutulc/overview

Uniform Law Commission, "Child Custody Jurisdiction and Enforcement Act," webpage, undated-b. As of November 28, 2022:
https://www.uniformlaws.org/committees/community-home?CommunityKey=4cc1b0be-d6c5-4bc2-b157-16b0baf2c56d

Uniform Law Commission, "Interstate Family Support Act," webpage, undated-c. As of November 28, 2022:
https://www.uniformlaws.org/committees/community-home?CommunityKey=71d40358-8ec0-49ed-a516-93fc025801fb

USAFAI—*See* U.S. Air Force Academy Instruction.

U.S. Air Force Academy, "Approved Budget Class of 2022 AY21-22," Department of the Air Force, undated. As of August 31, 2022:
Proposed Budget AY 21-22 Traditional.xlsx (usafa.edu)

U.S. Air Force Academy, *Demographic Profile of the Incoming USAFA Class of 2025*, July 8, 2021.

U.S. Air Force Academy, "Fall 2022 Semester Calendar," August 2022.

U.S. Air Force Academy Form 118, "Cadet Basic Allowance For Subsistence (BAS) Request," December 19, 2018.

U.S. Air Force Academy Instruction 36-2005, *Readmission of Former USAF Academy Cadets*, U.S. Air Force Academy, October 27, 2017, certified current May 27, 2021.

U.S. Air Force Academy Instruction 36-2007, *Application for and Administration of Cadet Turnback Program*, U.S. Air Force Academy, April 18, 2007, certified current December 9, 2020.

U.S. Air Force Academy Instruction 36-3504, *Disenrollment of United States Air Force Academy Cadets*, U.S. Air Force Academy, July 7, 2017.

U.S. Air Force Academy Instruction 36-3504, *Disenrollment of United States Air Force Academy Cadets*, U.S. Air Force Academy, August 15, 2022.

U.S. Code, Title 10, Armed Forces; Subtitle A, General Military Law; Part I, Organization and General Military Powers; Chapter 1, Definitions, Rules of Construction, Cross References, and Related Matters; Section 101, Definitions.

U.S. Code, Title 10, Armed Forces; Subtitle A, General Military Law; Part II, Personnel; Chapter 40, Leave; Section 702, Cadets and Midshipmen; Item C, Inapplicable Leave Provisions.

U.S. Code, Title 10, Armed Forces; Subtitle A, General Military Law; Part II, Personnel; Chapter 47, Uniform Code of Military Justice; Subchapter I, General Provisions; Section 802, Article 2: Persons Subject to This Chapter.

U.S. Code, Title 10, Armed Forces; Subtitle A, General Military Law; Part II, Personnel; Chapter 49, Miscellaneous Prohibitions and Penalties; Section 971, Service Credit: Officers May Not Count Service Performed While Serving as Cadet or Midshipman.

U.S. Code, Title 10, Armed Forces; Subtitle A, General Military Law; Part II, Personnel; Chapter 55, Medical and Dental Care.

U.S. Code, Title 10, Armed Forces; Subtitle B, Army; Part III, Training; Chapter 753, United States Military Academy; Section 7446, Cadets: Requirements for Admission.

U.S. Code, Title 10, Armed Forces; Subtitle B, Army; Part III, Training; Chapter 753, United States Military Academy; Section 7448, Cadets: Agreement to Serve as Officer.

U.S. Code, Title 10, Armed Forces; Subtitle C, Navy and Marine Corps; Part III, Education and Training; Chapter 853, United States Naval Academy; Section 8458, Midshipmen: Qualifications for Admission.

U.S. Code, Title 10, Armed Forces; Subtitle C, Navy and Marine Corps; Part III, Education and Training; Chapter 853, United States Naval Academy; Section 8459, Midshipmen: Agreement for Length of Service.

U.S. Code, Title 10, Armed Forces; Subtitle D, Air Force and Space Force; Part III, Training; Chapter 953, United States Air Force Academy; Section 9446, Cadets: Requirements for Admission.

U.S. Code, Title 10, Armed Forces; Subtitle D, Air Force and Space Force; Part III, Training; Chapter 953, United States Air Force Academy; Section 9448, Cadets: Agreement to Serve as Officer.

U.S. Code, Title 37, Pay and Allowances of the Uniformed Services; Chapter 3, Basic Pay; Section 203, Rates.

U.S. Code, Title 42, The Public Health and Welfare; Chapter 7, Social Security; Subchapter IV, Grant to State for Aid and Services to Needy Families with Children for Child Welfare Services; Part E, Federal Payments for Foster Care, Prevention, and Permanency.

U.S. Code, Title 50, War and National Defense; Chapter 50, Servicemembers Civil Relief; Sections 3901–4043.

U.S. Commandant of Cadets Policy Memorandum Number CC-20-12, *Procedures and Instructions in Cases of Cadet Pregnancies*, U.S. Military Academy, November 19, 2020.

U.S. Department of Defense, *Annual Report on Sexual Harassment and Violence at the Military Service Academies: Academic Program Year 2020–2021*, February 15, 2022.

U.S. Department of Justice, "Servicemembers Civil Relief Act Summary," webpage, December 13, 2021. As of November 28, 2022:
https://www.justice.gov/crt/servicemembers-civil-relief-act-summary

U.S. House of Representatives, National Defense Authorization Act for Fiscal Year 2022, Bill 4350, Section 559D, Requirement to Issue Regulations Ensuring Certain Parental Guardianship Rights of Cadets and Midshipmen, October 18, 2021.

U.S. Military Academy, "Standard Operating Procedures: U.S. Military Academy (USMA) Cadet Recoupment & Reimbursement," Department of the Army, June 26, 2019.

U.S. Military Academy, "Character Program (Goldbook), Academic Year 2020," Department of the Army, September 12, 2019.

U.S. Military Academy, "2020 Cost of Education for Public Law 96-357," March 22, 2021.

U.S. Military Academy, "Physical Program (Whitebook), Academic Year 2023," Department of the Army, March 22, 2022.

U.S. Military Academy, "Military Program (Greenbook), Academic Year 2023," Department of the Army, July 10, 2022.

U.S. Military Academy Form 5-50-B, "USMA Branch for Active Duty Service Obligation (ADSO) Contract: United States Military Academy Supplemental Cadet Service Agreement, Career Satisfaction Program (CSP)—Branch for ADSO," Department of the Army, March 2014.

USNA—*See* U.S. Naval Academy.

U.S. Naval Academy, "Midshipman Stipend and Annual Budget Book: Academic Year 2022–2023," Department of the Navy, May 19, 2022.

Vesneski, William, "State Law and the Termination of Parental Rights," *Family Court Review*, Vol. 49, No. 2, April 2011.

Wex database, "Clear and Convincing Evidence," Legal Information Institute, undated. As of November 28, 2022:
https://www.law.cornell.edu/wex/clear_and_convincing_evidence